All About Bikes
and
Bicycling

All About Bikes and Bicycling

by Max Alth

A BERKLEY MEDALLION BOOK
PUBLISHED BY
BERKLEY PUBLISHING CORPORATION

Illustrated by Ed Epstein

Published by arrangement with Hawthorn Books, Inc.

Library of Congress Catalog Card Number: 75-39250

SBN 425-02388-5

BERKLEY MEDALLION BOOKS are published by
Berkley Publishing Corporation
200 Madison Avenue
New York, N.Y. 10016

BERKLEY MEDALLION BOOKS ® TM 757,375

Printed in the United States of America

Berkley Medallion Edition, JULY, 1973

Contents

1. Learning to Ride   7
2. Safety   19
3. Bike Touring and Camping   29
4. Selecting Your Cycle   37
5. Care   65
6. Repairs   85
7. Tires   93
8. Wheels   117
9. Brakes   133
10. Pedals and Cranks   151
11. Chains and Chain Wheels   161
12. Derailleurs   171
13. Hub Gears   187
14. Head Sets, Handlebars, and Seats   195
15. Frames   205
    Appendix   211
    Index   216

To Char,
Sy,
Mish,
Archie,
Arabella,
and all other
devoted cyclists

CHAPTER 1

Learning to Ride

Anyone can ride a bicycle. If you have never ridden, it may seem as though cycling requires the balance of a tightrope walker, the muscle control of a ballet dancer, and nerves of steel. But this is far from the case. Anyone with sufficient balance to walk can cycle.

If you have never ridden, it is difficult to appreciate the gyroscopic stabilizing force exerted by the spinning wheels. Once the cycle is moving along, there is really no need to even think about keeping the machine vertical. Until you ride, you will not know how easy it is.

The effort required at low speeds over level ground and up gentle hills, if you have gearing, is less than that expended when walking at a much slower pace. When you want to rest, you simply stop pedaling and glide along.

Cycling is not limited by age or physical condition. If you can walk, you are strong enough to cycle. Of course long trips and racing are another matter. These should not be undertaken without a doctor's checkup any more than anyone should play touch football or soccer without first making certain of his physical condition.

As an exercise cycling is more exciting than walking or jogging. Cycling need not be any more strenuous than walking, unless you want it to be, but even at a moderate pace one's motion is faster by far than walking. You see more and sense more, simply because you do cover more ground—and there is the bonus of downhill. There is a lot of simple pleasure in just rolling down a grade, not pedaling, just watching the landscape go by.

Cycling is more fun than jogging when two are on the move. You can talk when cycling. It's kind of difficult to do that when jogging. Like jogging, however, cycling can be varied to suit the individual and mood. You can sprint on a cycle just as readily as you can when on foot, and cycling offers the combination of workout and trip. You can't really do that when jogging. One can cycle up the road for a dozen miles or so with a group of congenial companions, stop for a bit of a breather and perhaps a smidgen of lunch, and return at anyone's pace. This is hardly the normal activity of a group of joggers. Jogging isn't social.

LEARNING-BIKE SIZE IS IMPORTANT

Cycles are very personal. You will not be comfortable on a bike that does not suit your frame and does not reflect your personality and life-style, and you will not know exactly what to look for in a cycle until you have had some cycling experience under your belt.

The cycle on which you learn must be small enough to permit you to place both feet flat on the ground (see Figure 1) when you are sitting correctly and comfortably on the saddle. Preferably it should be a lady's

FIGURE 1. To learn without fear, you need a cycle that permits you to rest both feet flat on the ground.

bike with a dropped top tube or bar. It is easier to get down from a woman's cycle because of this feature. If you already have a cycle and you can lower its seat sufficiently to satisfy the feet-on-the-ground rule, fine. If not, rent or borrow a cycle.

Don't waste time and money on a set of training wheels for the youngster, unless he is not really ready to learn. Training wheels may help reduce the fear of falling, but no one learns to ride with them in place.

Don't give a child, or a small adult either, a large-sized bike with wood blocks taped to the pedals. This is frightening and dangerous because it requires a balancing act to stay vertical.

Check the bike out, as suggested in Chapter 5, to make certain it is in working order. Adjust the seat, or saddle as it is called, to a level position, that is, parallel with the ground. (You may want to change its angle after you learn, but a level position is best for starting out.)

Wear suitable clothes. No long skirts, no high heels, no toeless slippers, and no bare feet. If you are wearing trousers and there is no chain guard, roll them up or put on a trouser clip.

An experienced—though foolish—rider is inconvenienced when his pants become caught between the drive wheel and chain. A beginner will be knocked down and possibly seriously injured.

TAKING OFF

Find a level, empty stretch of road clear of obstructions. You cannot and should not hold on to anything while you are learning. A trusted friend at your side makes for good moral support, but he or she isn't necessary.

Sit your cycle, both feet touching the ground. Make yourself comfortable. If you have gears, select a middle speed. Now, with both feet still touching the ground, straighten your cycle, front wheel pointing ahead. Now lift both feet experimentally, just a little. For a second you will be balanced. Neither foot will touch the ground. Then you will tilt, but only a fraction of a degree because your foot will be right there. Bring your cycle to the vertical position again.

Repeat this little balancing act over and over. Each

time you lift your feet, lift them a bit higher. Wiggle your body slightly to hold your balance longer. Repeat the exercise until you know that you are not going to fall down and hurt or embarrass yourself when you lose balance and tilt. After a while you will surprise yourself by your ability to hold balance for five seconds or more. When you are able to do this, you are ready for the next step.

Place both feet on the ground, cycle upright. Push the cycle gently forward by pushing backward with the ball of one foot, then the other. This will feel awkward, because you must keep your legs spread apart to avoid striking the pedals. But you will be able to move slowly. As you move, you will tilt to one side. Turn your cycle a bit toward the side to which you are falling. Soon you will learn to automatically wriggle your handlebars to keep your balance. After a while you will coast along without needing to touch either foot to the ground for quite a distance. Rest. Get off the cycle, walk about a bit. Sit down, accept congratulations, have a beer. But rest.

Repeat the exercise several times, resting every so often. Don't overdo it. Pushing this way is an unusual physical action. You may stiffen up. And you will get tired, especially if you are over twenty-one and have a healthy, normal fear of falling.

Hold your bike upright with one hand, and operate the pedals with your other hand, rolling it forward until the right-hand pedal (your right leg rests on it when you are sitting on the cycle) is a little past the high point. Seat the cycle. Lean all the way forward. Place your right foot on the right pedal; your left foot on the ground. Put some of your weight on the right pedal, and push backward with your left foot. See Figure 2. You will now roll forward, one leg trailing behind. Hold your balance as long as you can, turning the cycle a little to the right and left to keep yourself from falling.

11

FIGURE 2. Take-off position for beginners: left foot on the ground, ready to push; right foot on the pedal, ready to press down; body low and forward over the handlebars.

Stop when you have lost your forward momentum. If the pedal is not in the correct position, place it in the correct position. Repeat this exercise again and again.

After a dozen repeated half-pedals or so, you will find that you will be able to go for a considerable distance and that you will have plenty of time to place your left foot on the left pedal. When you have reached this point, do not wait until your forward momentum decays, but simply start pedaling slowly. Straighten up a bit and continue to pedal. Courage, *mon capitaine*—keep your head up and look to the future. Don't look down at the wheel; you may become dizzy.

Turning is easy; just point the front wheel in the

direction you wish to go. Should you find that you are losing your balance, stop and place your feet on the ground. When you get more confidence and more experience, you will find that balance improves with speed. The faster you go, the easier it is to keep your balance.

Avoid hills, narrow roads, obstacles, and the like while you are learning. Your balance is not good, and you will be in trouble if you suddenly meet a new experience. Just pedal around and around your training area. Try right and left turns. Don't take up the challenge to go out on the road or to race. Stay in the middle or low gear.

Braking is easy but requires a bit of caution at first. If you have hand brakes, tape a block of wood beneath the left-hand brake lever—the lever that works the front-wheel brakes—so that you cannot accidentally stop your front wheel while learning. Don't worry; you have plenty of braking action in the rear brake alone.

The front-wheel brake is always energized a moment after the rear-wheel hand-brake lever is squeezed. If not, if the front wheel is braked before the rear wheel, you will skid to one side at low speed and possibly flip at high speed. So to make certain you do not squeeze the wrong lever at the wrong time, it is taped out of action. Later you can free it.

If you have coaster brakes, there will normally be no hand-brake levers on the handle bars—though some bikes are equipped with both. Coaster brakes are kicked in by back-pedaling when you want to stop. You feel the brake take hold when you have backed the pedals about half a turn. The more reverse pressure you apply, the more quickly the wheel comes to a stop.

With experience you will learn to automatically adjust brake pressure to speed and road conditions. You will learn to lean back to get more weight on the rear wheel when stopping. It all comes with practice.

13

Dismounting is accomplished by reversing the steps taken to mount. The cycle is slowed down, but not to a complete stop unless you want everyone to know you are a beginner. Right-handers lift the left leg up and behind them, swinging it back over the seat and bringing it down and parallel and slightly behind the right leg. The body is upright, and the bike is in the tilt position. If this is done with finesse, the cycle will come to a stop at the instant the left foot touches the ground.

There is another dismount sequence, which is very useful when your brakes fail. Again, for right-handers: Take your feet from both pedals. Lift your left leg up and over the bar, or through the gap if you are riding a woman's cycle. Place your left foot on the right pedal. Tilt the cycle, and stand up. Now rest your right shoe sole, not toe, on the ground. Drag your sole, applying more weight until you come to a stop.

Riding comfort, once you have learned how, is mainly common sense. You will be using different muscles from walking or running, and as a beginner you must expect to tire easily. Rest by getting off the cycle and walking till you cool down.

Riding ease is greatly dependent on your cycle and how you sit it. Figure 3 illustrates the correct and incorrect riding positions. Position A is entirely too erect. You cannot pump effectively from this position. You will tire quickly and lack power, because only a portion of the leg muscles can be brought to bear on the pedals.

Position B is correct for ordinary, everyday cycling. The back forms a forty-five-degree angle or so with the top bar. Approximately 20 percent of the body's weight is carried by the arms, and approximately 25 percent of the weight is carried by the legs. Arms and legs are easily rested from time to time by straightening up and by bending the knees. There is no exact guide for body angle and weight distribution in the cruising position. Each rider experiments until he finds what is best for

FIGURE 3. Correct and incorrect riding positions. Position A is entirely too erect. B is a good compromise position for everyday pedaling. Position C is most comfortable for the long-distance, experienced cyclist.

himself. Seat angle, handlebar position, seat-to-pedal distance, and frame shape, size, and design all affect body position, riding efficiency, and comfort. That is why it is wise to postpone cycle purchase until you know what you want.

The third position, C, is for the experienced cyclist. It will vary with individual riders from the forty-five-degree back angle suited for cruising, all the way down to an almost horizontal back position favored by racers. There will be much more weight on the arms and a little more on the legs. Generally the racer wants to move himself a bit forward of the pedal crank. The seat may be tilted more severely downward.

With ordinary pedals you propel yourself by pushing straight down on the pedals. For greater efficiency one uses toe clips plus foot straps, which are equipped with quick-disconnect features (like ski bindings they give way under pressure).

Beginners should never use clips and bindings. They are not to be used by anyone who expects to fall down. It takes skill and experience to remove one's foot in a hurry from shoe clips and straps. Their value lies in increased pumping efficiency. Without the clips you can only press downward. With the clips you can pull up as well as push down. All racers and cross-country riders use them. The difference in power and speed is marked. Toe clips and straps also let you use your ankles when pumping, and this too adds to your speed.

SHIFTING

A beginner should not attempt to shift until he has mastered cycling in one gear fairly well. If the beginner's cycle does have gears, select a gear ratio of sixty, which will be the middle gear on a three-speed cycle, or use the lower speed, which may be forty-five or fifty on a two-speed cycle. Cycling is easier for a beginner at slow speed. The meaning of the numbers with which various cycle gear speeds are identified is explained in Chapter 4 under "Gear Ratio." It should be noted that gears, that is, speed changers, are not a necessity but a convenience. In flat country there is little need for them at all.

There are two types of gear changers: hub types and

derailleur types. The hub type is identified by a small chain emerging from the center of the hub. The derailleur is identified by the cluster of gears on the rear hub and the extra length of chain traveling over a set of rollers. Suffice it to say here, so far as the beginner is concerned, both are satisfactory but are operated differently, and if operated improperly they can be damaged just like the gears in a car.

You can safely shift a hub changer when both the rear wheel and the pedals are immobile and when the rear wheel is overrunning the pedals. Put another way: You are pumping along with a hub changer and want to shift up or down; you hold your pedals steady, the chain stops moving, the bike continues to roll. You shift and start pumping again. The actual shift is accomplished by moving the little shift lever.

To safely shift a derailleur, the following sequence of steps is necessary. You pump along as before. When you want to shift, you ease up on your pumping—but you do not stop moving the pedals completely—then you shift. This is done by slowly moving a lever, which is usually mounted on the frame. After shifting you pump again. You cannot have pressure on the chain when you shift, because it will strain the chain wheel and bend it, and you cannot hold your feet still, because the derailleur will not work. Actually the derailleur just pushes the chain from one sprocket wheel to another.

Practice shifting so that you can do it smoothly and you do not forget and chip some teeth from a sprocket.

CHAPTER 2

Safety

It has been said, with more accuracy than humor, that safety is no accident. This is very true. There are many factors affecting our lives over which we have little control, but only a fool believes all is Kismet—fate. You can no more cross a busy highway at night with your eyes closed and survive than you can jump from a tall building and avoid making a splash.

The fewer risks you take, the better your chances of reaching old age in fairly good working order, and you reduce risks by planning ahead for contingencies and by developing safe, sensible habits. All this may sound overly cautious, formal, and time-consuming, but once you consider all the situations in advance, once you have developed and instituted your program, it becomes automatic. You do the right thing at the right time without hesitancy, fear, or loss of time.

Develop the habit of observing the road directly in front of your bike as you roll along. Look out for potholes, cracks, bumps, and the like. Watch out for storm sewer covers with long slots that can catch your wheel. Keep out of trolley tracks; some of them are still around. If you get in, stop and pick the cycle up and out. If you have to cross tracks, do so at a sharp angle.

Be wary of dust, sand, and leaves when going around turns. Any of these can cause you to slip. Avoid puddles, if you can. If you can't, apply your brakes lightly after passing through. This will remove the water from your brakes, so they will work properly and effectively when you need them.

OBEY THE LAW

Cycles are covered by the road laws of the various states. As a cyclist, you must keep to the right and obey all traffic signals and signs. Your cycle must have a front light, a rear reflector, and a horn or audible sounding device. Specifics vary from state to state. New York State, for example, requires a state-approved reflector and a light capable of being seen for a distance of five hundred feet ahead or two hundred feet when viewed by an oncoming motorist with his bright lights on.

A cyclist must signal turns just like a motorist. Figure 4 shows you the signals: left hand fully extended and horizontal for a left-hand turn; hand and arm in a vertical position for a right-hand turn; hand down and a little to the left for a stop.

Left turn   Right turn   Stop

FIGURE 4. A cyclist must signal turns just like a motorist.

SAFETY IN TRAFFIC

Beware of the motorist. Stay to the extreme right of the road. Ride in single file when traveling in a group. Obey all traffic signals and signs. This is emphasized for your own protection.

Don't be a wise guy. Don't use the agility of your cycle to slip through files of autos poised at a stop light. They may not see you when the light changes. Should your route take you across a busy intersection that is not fully protected by lights, walk your cycle.

Stay out of fast traffic. For a cyclist this is anything more than eighteen miles per hour. Automobiles will be concerned only with other autos, and some of the idiots will pull up beside you, sharing a single lane.

Don't tailgate moving cars. They can stop much more quickly than you can.

Watch those parked cars. People sometimes step out abruptly from between them. Motorists frequently leave their cars illegally by the road-side door.

Be very careful going around turns on narrow roads. Watch carefully for oncoming traffic, especially at blind turns and sharp hilltops. Your side of the road may be clear, but some idiot may be passing from the other direction on the blind turn. You may meet him head-on. By keeping to the side, you will give him room to pass. By the same thought, don't get caught to one side of a car going around a blind turn. If the aforementioned idiot comes barreling over to your side of the road, the car on your side will automatically shift to its right. The driver will flinch before the oncoming car, and before he even thinks about what's to his right, he will have pushed you off the road. Of course, if there is a group of you, don't spread wide going around a blind turn.

Learn to listen for oncoming cars when traveling narrow country roads. Farmers are wild drivers. They usually shoot right down the middle. When you do hear a car up ahead on a narrow road, look behind you. The sound of the oncoming car may be masking the sound of a second or even third car coming from behind. The sound may be reflecting from trees or buildings. There may be only one automobile, and that may not be ahead of you—though it sounds that way.

Watch your speed. You can hit forty going downhill; try to stop on a wet or dusty road and you'll skid a mile.

Obviously, the safest place to cycle is on cycle-only paths and sidewalks when no pedestrians are abroad. Back roads are very pleasurable and safe but sometimes lead to carelessness because of the infrequent appearance of automobiles. When touring such roads in a group, establish a leader-follower plan of action so that on the sound of an oncoming auto the group will form a safe, single file without confusion or waste of time.

DON'T RIDE AT NIGHT

If you must cycle at night, make sure your light is in working order and the battery is fresh. Generator lights are good, because they don't need attention: There are no batteries to forget to replace. However, they cease to function when you slow down and stop. So generator lights are of no value when you walk the cycle or stop for a moment at the side of the road. Should your light fail, get off your bike and walk it along the edge of the road against traffic.

Be certain you have a reflector in the rear. It is good safety practice to add a second reflector. Place it on your tool bag or on the pedals or panniers.

If the traffic is heavy and/or the weather is bad, get off the road altogether. On bad nights, motorists have difficulty seeing the road. On any night, they work on the theory that no one would be stupid enough to be on the road. Some may look hard into the shadows, concerned with pedestrians, cyclists, and small beasties. But after they have looked into a dozen bright lights, after they have driven for some time, the most conscientious drivers become numb. And bright lights hypnotize. Just stay out of the motorist's way.

BAD WEATHER

Avoid cycling in bad weather. Safety is as simple as that. Cycles slip, and so do automobiles. Visibility is reduced, and the danger from automobiles is multiplied. If you must go out during rain, let a little air out of the tires. This will give you more rubber on the ground and more traction.

Don't hitch a ride behind a truck. It will get up speed far more quickly than you imagine. Should you hit a bump, you will be thrown from your cycle. When you let go at thirty or forty miles per hour, the blast of air that hits you when you get out from the partial vacuum behind the truck will probably knock you down. In traffic you will be invisible to the second and following cars behind the truck you are hitching. And should the truck make a fast turn or stop, you will be thrown or worse.

Don't horse around. Stunt riding has its place, but it is not on public roads. Don't push or pull on another cyclist while he is on his bike. Don't carry someone on your handlebars, or let him ride on your seat while you stand up and pedal, or otherwise overload the bike by tying heavy packages on it. There is little danger the cycle will be damaged directly. It is tough enough to carry another hundred pounds or so. But you will lose control. You will wobble badly going up hills and may simply lose balance and fall when it is most dangerous. Most states forbid two people on a bike made for one. Get a tandem if you want to go double.

Don't jump the curb. This is the practice of driving directly over the curbstone and onto the sidewalk. If the curb is just a little too high, you may stop dead and go head over tipsy. If you do not strike the curbstones full square, your front wheel may slip to one side and you will fall against and across the curbstone. At best you will damage your front tire and wheel. This may or may not be immediately apparent, but damage will be done, and the wheel will wobble very quickly.

Some wise alecks lift the front wheel when they jump the curb. This saves the front end of your bike, but the rear wheel still has to get over the barrier. If you throw your weight forward onto the handlebars at just the right instant, you may get away without damaging your rear wheel. Then again, you may go down in a heap All it takes is a little water, dust, pebble, or miscalculation.

HEALTH PRECAUTIONS

Cycling is not particularly strenuous if done in moderation. However, if you are in ill health, if there is any doubt as to the condition of your heart, see the doctor first.

If you are basically sound but merely out of condition, cycling is an excellent means of exercise, when done with caution. Try to cycle a little each day. Slow down when you begin to puff. Stop well before you reach the end of your rope. Overexertion destroys tissue. Strain followed by rest builds muscle tissue. After a while you will be able to sense when you should rest. If you break your exercise period into short sessions, you will find that it is more fun, that you can do more and more each time.

Go easy on the food before cycling. Too much food will make you logy and possibly fill you with gas. Should this happen, stop and try pulling your stomach in and releasing it. If you are racing and cannot stop, shove your fist into your stomach to break up the gas and help you release pressure.

If you are expecting some hard and fast riding—an uphill sprint, for example—and feel you must eat, avoid milk and milk products. Avoid foods that are hard to digest—rich gravies, pizza, and other foods that combine oils and starches—and drink a minimum of liquids.

If you are planning a long trip, bring along fruit juice, wine, or beer. These will give you an immediate lift. Stay away from soda pop. If you must have pop, drink it warm and shake it to release the gas.

When you are hot, do not drink cold water; it may give you cramps. Whether you are hot from exertion or temperature, it is best to drink lukewarm liquids. If you must drink cold, sip. Do not drink ice-cold soda. The gas will be suddenly released within your gullet and double you up with pain. On a very hot day hot tea with sugar is very refreshing.

On cold days cover up when you stop cycling. If you happen to be wearing a sweater or jacket, don't remove it when you stop. The cold air may stiffen you like a board.

WEAR SUITABLE CLOTHING

If you plan to stop during your trip, bring along a sweater or jacket to keep you warm when you are not cycling. If the weather is cold, bring along trousers to slip on over your shorts.

Your clothing should be loose. Not so loose that it flaps in the wind and acts as a drag or catches in the chain or wheels, but loose enough to permit free circulation.

Do not wear garters, girdles, tight sweaters that make you sigh with relief when you remove them, or stockings with rubber tops. All body pressure reduces blood flow and acts as a physical load. If you cut circulation badly enough, you will get a charley horse (cramp) in that member when you become tired.

Underclothing, if worn, should be of cotton. Only cotton absorbs perspiration. All the synthetics are moisture-proof, and you will soon be sopping wet and uncomfortable. Sweaters and jackets should be of wool. Most synthetics are not warm. The exceptions are padded ski jackets or the ski shells over sweaters. Trousers should be loose, preferably all cotton, because the synthetics will irritate your legs. They are cold and become clammy when you perspire, for they neither absorb nor transport moisture.

Avoid tight ski pants. Even loosely fitting ski pants can be a terrible load, because they contain rubber, which resists body movement. They may look good if you have the legs for them, but they are a heavy burden when pedaling.

CHAPTER 3

*Bike Touring
and Camping*

Group cycle touring or cycle hiking is an adventure. When it is well planned, it will be a pleasure; when it is not—well—there can be many uncomfortable moments.

Given sufficient knowledge, proper preparation and equipment, and mature adventurers, a nine-month tour of the Canadian Rockies or a five-hour run to the local falls and back can be pure pleasure. If all is left to chance and luck blows the other way, there will be dozens of "I told you so's" and lots of tears.

Some of the major points to consider before rolling off to the blue horizon are as follows.

DON'T MIX YOUR BAG

There is hardly anything more irritating than forced association with a group of cyclists who are either much faster or much slower than yourself. A prime consideration in planning any trip, therefore, is to make certain that the cyclists are of equal capability, stamina, and interest and have reasonably identical cycles.

There is nothing wrong with bringing little children along in child carriers. The kids are safe and comfortable, but the parents hauling the little brats may be more heavily laden than the balance of the party and will fall behind. Even if Dad keeps up by heroic effort, the kid will not sit still the many hours an adult cyclist may want to pedal without stopping.

The same is true of the very young and the very old. A ten- or twelve-year-old child can probably pedal as long and as fast as many adults, but most often the children lose interest and want to stop long before they are really tired. A seventy-year-old can be just as selfish.

Equipment must also be given careful evaluation. If some of the wheels have low gears and the others do not, there will be dissatisfaction on the hills. Those who can gear up the hills will not want to wait for those who have to walk up to the top.

HAVE AN OBJECTIVE

There is something in almost all humans that makes "unstructured" play disappointing and unsatisfying. Ask any five fellow cyclists to just wheel about for an afternoon, and they will most likely refuse to join you. Suggest that the same group cycle to the local police station to read the police blotter of the previous night, or to the river to slug rats, or to the end of Route 67, or what have you, and you may have a fierce argument, but eventually there will be a happy group with a common objective.

So when planning a group cycle, pick a target. If it's to be a full day's outing, pick one or two targets, one for noon and one for later in the day. If several days are to be spent on the road, plan several objectives for each day. For example, should you plan to do one hundred miles on a particular day, select your lunch stop before setting out. Pack a lunch, or ascertain that a meal can be purchased at the halfway mark.

DON'T OVERREACH

Experienced cyclists may welcome a long run as a challenge. Others will not. They prefer ample time to rest and sightsee along the way. A few in your party may be annoyed by overly long rests or too frequent stops. But ask the same individuals to exceed their usual degree of physical exertion, and they will scream. Put more simply: It is a far wiser leader who underrates his charges than the one who overrates them. Study the terrain, and plan on quitting for the evening at four or even earlier, rather than at six. You'll find your little group pedaling along till six often enough without planning it that way.

CAMP OR TOUR?

According to the more-or-less accepted definition of the two terms, camping means to sleep outdoors under shelter carried for the purpose. Touring means traveling from one commercial inn or hotel to another, having meals prepared by others, and sleeping under a man-made roof hired for the night.

Obviously it is far less sporting to buy your meals and lodging, far simpler, and less taxing. What may not be as obvious is that camping is loads more fun when you have proper equipment and an experienced guide—Dad will do fine.

When you camp, you are free. You can go where

others rarely go. The cycle gives you the physical reach impractical to back-packers and enables you to follow paths inaccessible to automobiles. Because almost everyone in the country rides in an automobile, and thousands of motorized campers are sold every year, your cycle will take you just about as far out of sight of your fellow man as you may wish to go.

In addition to your cycle you will need perhaps fifty dollars per person for camping gear that will last years and years. Each individual will need a lightweight sleeping bag, or a large one for doubles, plus a tent for each pair, lightweight cooking gear, and for the less hardy an air mattress and assorted items of smaller gear. Several good books and some excellent mail-order camping supply houses are listed at the end of this book.

If you are touring, it is advisable to make reservations well in advance. And if you wish, send your gear on ahead. Just inform the management it is coming.

If you plan to camp, considerably more preparation is required. To me, anyway, this is a large part of the fun. You and your little group are going to carry everything on your cycles. Your objective will be to take everything you may need in the wilds without overloading. Forty pounds per cycle is just about maximum load, so the logistics are far from simple. Incidentally, don't carry anything in back packs. They are uncomfortable and place too much weight up too high for easy balance. Get panniers.

Camping is luxurious and comfortable for those with woodsmanship and proper equipment. In the city the country bumpkin gets lost and into trouble. In the deep woods it's the city fellow that gets stung, wet, and uncomfortable, because he doesn't know where to pitch his tent or protect himself against black flies and the little animals that steal his grub. The inexperienced woodsman will be wise to take to the woods gradually, combining touring with camping, limiting his overnights in the forest to an evening at a time, and never straying too far from help, otherwise known as civilization.

There is a low-cost compromise between touring and camping that is well worth considering. It is called hosteling.

Hostels are homes, barns, schools, churches, and even castles and mountain lodges (in Europe) that have special facilities for overnight accommodations for travelers. Many of the hostels are operated by their owners, who take considerable pride in their establishment. There are two hundred hostels in forty-seven countries. The charge per person per night ranges from one to three dollars.

You are advised to reserve space in advance and to arrive between five and seven in the evening. Hostelers are expected to get to bed at a reasonable hour, to arise early, and to leave the establishment by about nine A.M. Stays at any one hostel are limited to three nights, with extended stays possible by special permission.

With a few exceptions hostel sleeping accommodations are limited to dorms for men and women. There are a few that are prepared for married folk. Smoking in the dorms and alcoholic beverages are prohibited.

The hostel provides bunks, blankets, facilities, and cleaning equipment. Although you are expected to have your own sleeping sack (two bed sheets sewn together on three sides), you can rent clean sheets from the hostel manager. Many hostels provide a common kitchen and dining room where hostelers may cook their own meals using hostel cooking equipment. Some hostels have their own cooking staff and offer cheap but substantial meals. Everything is self-service, and you are expected to clean up after yourself if you cook. Very often there are organized work details.

Hostelers are expected to arrive by foot, horseback,

canoe, cycle, dogsled, or skis. Motor campers are not encouraged; neither are ordinary motorists if they are traveling during peak season.

For admission, you must have a Youth Hostel membership card, which is good the world over. (See listing at the end of this book for addresses of local AYH offices.) The cost of a membership card is five dollars for those under eighteen and ten dollars for those over eighteen. There is no age limit, so don't be put off by the word "youth."

With your membership you will receive a brochure listing all the hostels plus additional hosteling information and the American Youth Hostel publication, *The Hosteler*. AYH is a nonprofit, nonsectarian corporation. Its purpose is charitable and educational, with emphasis on promoting a greater understanding of the world and its people through low-cost travel and outdoor activities. AYH sponsors many kinds of field trips comprising small groups traveling with a trained leader. These include cycle hikes both here and abroad, which may be as long as a single afternoon or several weeks.

TOURING FOR CITY DWELLERS

To someone living in the eastern or western megalopolis the possibility of finding any unused back road appears preposterously small. We city denizens have often driven all day without being quit of a covey of motor cars and trucks for a single instant. It may not be easy to believe, but out there amid all those giant, magnificent superhighways lies a considerable number of small, untraveled byways.

Since we almost always travel to cover distance, we follow the shortest, fastest path. And these roads are the most traveled. The trick to finding quiet roads suitable for cycling is to examine local maps and actually drive down roads you have never followed before.

Communities are building cycle paths; ask your local recreation department. Cycle clubs know where the quiet, safe roads are; contact your local cycle clubs, or call your local newspaper. They are usually aware of all civic group activities.

When time permits, you can transport your cycle to a quiet lane. There are carriers available for mounting cycles on one's automobile. And if you reverse a cycle's pedals and remove its handlebars and front wheel, it can be packed into a comparatively small space.

There are also many folding cycles on the market.

A bibliography of books and other sources of cycle travel information is located at the end of this book.

CHAPTER 4

*Selecting
Your Cycle*

Choosing the correct cycle is like choosing the correct shoe. It must fit you, and it must fit the occasion.

TYPES OF CYCLES

There are cycles designed and manufactured expressly for delivering, hacking, touring, road racing, track racing, old folk (tricycles), kids, and people who want to carry their wheels in the luggage compartment of their automobiles (folding cycles).

Cycle prices range from as low as $50 to well over $350. Used cycles can fetch as little as $5 in working condition to as much as three-quarters the original purchase price when in good or excellent condition.

Delivery cycles are heavy and tough. They usually

have small front wheels over which giant baskets are suspended. Some delivery cycles are tricycles with a large basket mounted between two parallel wheels. Delivery cycles are intended for hauling. Don't make the error of purchasing one for pleasure riding.

Hacking cycles are used for "hacking" about, running errands, leaving at the railroad station when you go into town, riding along the beach. They cost about fifty dollars and may weigh as many pounds. They are tough, useful, and durable. As a first cycle for a child they are excellent.

Experienced cyclists call them American bombers, ice wagons—that was years ago—or trucks. Generally they come equipped with balloon tires. Bombers are long on wear but tough on the legs. In recent years cycles in this class have been modified—hopped up is a better description—with very high handlebars, V-shaped back rests, imitation motors, complex front springing, and long double seats designed to support two young bottoms. (Double seats are extremely dangerous when two are riding, because control is very poor.)

Touring cycles are lighter, faster, more beautiful, and more expensive than the hacking or general-duty cycles. Touring cycles will not stand up to the abuse expected to be meted out to hacking cycles. Touring cycles should not be exposed to rain, salt air, potholes, bumps, or dirt.

Touring cycles weigh in at twenty-five to thirty pounds or so. There is no definite break-off point between the general-duty bike and the tourer except weight, though the tour wheel usually has hand brakes whereas the hack frequently comes with a coaster brake. Touring bikes cost from seventy-five to two hundred dollars.

If you plan to take to the back woods and expect rough going, select a heavier cycle, say thirty pounds, with thicker, lower-pressure tires. The heavier bike will

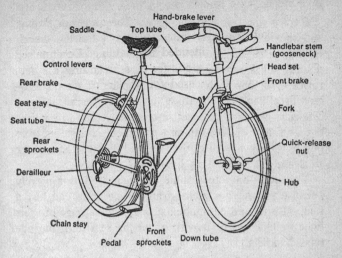

Hand-brake lever

Saddle   Top tube

Handlebar stem
(gooseneck)

Control levers   Head set

Rear brake   Front brake

Seat stay

Seat tube   Fork

Rear
sprockets   Quick-release
                                  nut

Derailleur   Hub

Chain stay

Pedal   Front   Down tube
         sprockets

FIGURE 5. Major parts of a touring cycle with fixed-gear drive.

stand up to obstacles better and give you a more comfortable ride.

Racing cycles look like touring cycles. The basic difference is weight and cost. Anything under 25 pounds
can be classed as a racer. Some are slimmed down to
less than 20 pounds. Racers cost from $150 to well
over $350, and more.

Racing cycle designers strive for strength without
weight. They select the strongest metals, then cut back
on weight by making the tubing thick at the ends, where
maximum load occurs, and thin in the middle, the area
of minimum load. This is called double butting and is
explained in detail in the chapter on frames. The better
the cycle, the closer the designer has come to the line
that divides speed and collapse. Spills that merely
remove a little paint from the frame of a hacking wheel
can spell the end of the road for an expensive, high-

speed, lightweight racer. This is something to be considered when selecting a cycle.

Racers are fast and beautiful. They are not strong, and they are not as comfortable as a touring wheel. Racing tires are generally pumped to one hundred pounds per square inch (psi) or more. The tires are narrower, only one inch wide. (Tour bikes run on 1 1/4-inch tires, hacks on anything from 1 3/8 inches on up.) The narrow, hard tires roll more easily than other tires but do skid more readily and jar much more going over bumps. They are also thinner and lighter than other tires and do not last as long.

You don't have to assume the racing position merely because you have a racing-frame cycle. You can buy a racing frame and components to take advantage of their light weight, but fit it with a touring seat and touring-type handlebars.

BIKE SIZE

Cycling comfort and efficiency depend on matching the cyclist's little body to his or her machine. You can no more pedal with speed and pleasure on a bike of the wrong size than you can win a dance contest in undersized shoes.

The size of a bike is determined by its frame. Wheel size has little to do with it, though obviously you cannot put sixteen-inch wheels on a frame designed for twenty-eight-inch wheels.

You may hear salesmen say, "Buy a small-wheel bike for a kid, a bike with a big wheel for an adult." They may also state out of honest ignorance that there is no such thing as a choice of frame sizes. This is commonly heard in discount houses, department stores, and hardware shops and is probably true; generally these places do not specialize in cycles but simply offer good, low-priced bikes in a choice of colors and wheel sizes only. Therefore it makes good sense to patronize a cycle shop. Some of them have been in business for more than one hundred years. They know what they are talking about; they stock parts and have experienced bike repairmen on hand.

Just as there are two shoe dimensions that cannot be ignored, there are also two bike dimensions that cannot be ignored. In a shoe it is length and width. In a cycle it is frame size and reach. These and other cycle dimensions are illustrated in Figure 6.

The distance between one's bottom and the pedals is determined by frame size. This is measured in inches from the center of the crank hanger (center of the chain wheel) to the top of the seat post—not the top of the seat.

If the frame size is too large for the cyclist, he or she will not be able to reach the pedal at the bottom of its swing. This is what happens when kids ride an adult cycle. They have to stand up and swing from side to side

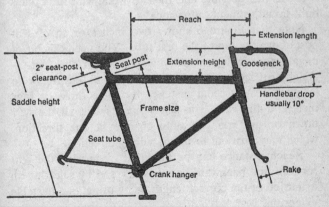

FIGURE 6. Major frame dimensions.

as they pedal. This is dangerous, because it is difficult to control the cycle from this position. Taping blocks of wood to the pedals is equally dangerous and should not be done.

If the cyclist is very tall and the frame is short, his knees will come up to his chin—elbows at the very least—and an equally uncomfortable, dangerous condition will exist.

Frame sizes run from nineteen to twenty-four inches, so it is possible to find a frame for almost everybody.

The second bike dimension of major importance is reach. This is the distance from the front of the seat to the beginning of the handlebars, where they join the gooseneck or extension. If the reach on the cycle is too short, a tall individual will find his elbows in his ribs. If a short rider mounts a bike with an overly long reach, he will find himself stretching uncomfortably forward and carrying too much weight on his arms and back.

It is not crucial that frame and reach sizes fit the cyclist exactly. The trick is to choose a frame as close to perfect as possible and then to work with the cycle's built-in adjustment allowance.

Note that Figure 6 shows two inches or so of seat post above the top of the seat tube. You need this bit of metal showing to enable you to shorten the seat-to-pedal distance by two inches, if you so desire, or to lengthen seat-to-pedal distance by some three or four inches. If the cycle you select has its seat all the way down or up, you can only change in one direction, which may turn out to be the wrong direction.

Reach distance can be modified by moving the seat forward and backward as necessary and by selecting an extension of the correct length or by using an adjustable extension.

Now that we know what we are looking for in bike size, how do we go about finding the correct size?

There are two routes. One is simple. Measure your-

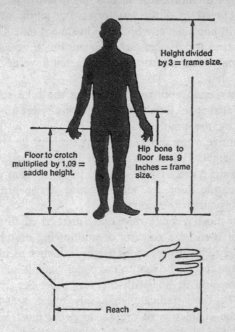

FIGURE 7. Computing frame size, saddle height, and reach.

self against the cycle of your choice. Put the shoe on and walk a bit. See if it fits.

Make certain the bike's tires are properly inflated and that you have at least two inches of seat post clearance. Seat the cycle. You should be able to touch both toes to the floor simultaneously. If you can't, the bike is too large. If you can sit flat-footed, the bike is too small. Remember, you don't want to give up your "adjustment," because you may want to make a change after you have ridden awhile.

Try pedaling. How is the reach? Are you comfortable? Do your knees get in the way of your arms? Again, you want to feel comfortable with the seat in the

43

center of the horizontal section of the seat post. If it has to be moved up all the way forward or all the way back, you will not have any further adjustment left. The same holds true for the handlebar extension. If you need an extremely long or short extension, you have no "adjustment" left.

The second approach to finding the bike size to fit your attractive little frame is more interesting. It is done by the numbers.

Remove your shoes, stand up straight, and measure your height. Divide this number by three, and you will have your correct frame size. Or measure from your hip bone to the floor, and subtract nine. Or measure from your crotch to the floor.

The most recently developed method of finding the correct cycle size consists of multiplying crotch height by 1.09. This gives saddle height in inches as measured from the top of the seat to the pedal when it is in its low position and in line with the seat tube. See Figures 6 and 7. Tests indicate that this exact seat-to-pedal distance enables most cyclists to pedal most efficiently and thus with least effort and highest speed.

To find reach, simply measure the distance from the tips of your outstretched fingers to your elbow.

FRAMES

The frame is the backbone of the machine. Almost everything else can be changed, but the frame cannot without literally changing cycles. The frame is the most expensive and important component of any bike.

Low-priced frames are sturdy, heavy, and unyielding. The better frames are lighter in weight, more flexible, and weaker. You can judge a frame to some extent by lifting it to measure its weight, rapping it with your finger, and listening for the presence or absence of the ringing sound typical of good steel. Sometimes you can flex a section in your hand by pulling on the top bar and pressing downward with your foot on the crank's central hub.

Inexpensive frames are simply tubes welded together. The better frames are joined by lugs. The lugs are more carefully joined on the better frames. The edge of each lug is cleaner; one can see the joining metal as a solid, smooth line—no roughness, no missing areas. Lugs are either silver-soldered or brazed at low temperature, 850° F. or so. High-temperature brazing makes the metal brittle.

The best bike-frame material is Reynolds 531, cold-drawn, seamless manganese-molybdenum steel. The best bike frames are made of double-butted Reynolds 531. Double-butting is a process that makes the tubing thicker at its ends, the point of maximum stress, and thinner along its central section where the stress is lower. Double-butting is not visible on the outside of the tubing; you can sometimes tell by sounding the tube with your finger.

All the tubes on a bike may or may not be double-

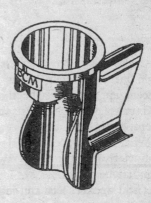

FIGURE 8. Lug.

butted, so there are three frame types you may encounter, all of Reynolds 531: the non-double-butted frame, the partially double-butted frame, and the top of the road, the completely double-butted frame. When a manufacturer goes to the cost and trouble of double-butting, you can be certain his bike carries the message; it is clearly labeled so.

If you are shopping for used frames, be sure to examine them carefully for alignment. Look down the length of the tubes to see if they are straight. Beware of frames with kinks. These indicate the tube was bent and straightened; such frames are usually weak at this point. Avoid frames with mangled lugs. These frames have been taken apart and resoldered. They could be excellent, but then again, the balance of the frame may be damaged. Gentle curves in the frame spoil its appearance but generally do not seriously weaken it.

Look for paint damage by heat. This indicates that a torch has been put to the metal, possibly to straighten it. Look for very rough paint areas. This can indicate that a heat-treated area has been crudely painted over to hide torch marks. Frames with indications of this kind of repair work are risky.

WHEELS

Cycles today have wheels from sixteen to twenty-eight inches in diameter as measured across the rim. Racers appear to prefer the twenty-eight-inch wheel, and many touring cyclists choose the relatively new twenty-seven-inch wheel.

What effect does wheel size have on the riding characteristics of a cycle? Why choose one wheel size over another?

The larger wheels are easier to propel, although if over twenty-eight inches, the increase in efficiency appears to fall off. This may be due to the greater weight and wind resistance of the larger wheel.

Smaller wheels are slightly more difficult to drive because the angle at which the circumference strikes an obstruction is greater than when the same obstruction contacts a larger wheel.

On the other hand, smaller wheels make for a smaller, lighter bike. The cyclist does not sit much closer to the ground, but the smaller wheels give many people the feeling of greater safety. Smaller-wheeled cycles are easier to pack into the back of the wagon and make smaller packages when incorporated into folding cycles. On a backwoods trail the smaller bike with the smaller wheels is often easier to push around obstructions and more easily maneuvered between obstacles.

Both steel and aluminum are used for wheel construction. If you go to aluminum, specify stainless-steel spoke, because ordinary steel and aluminum make a highly rust-prone combination.

Wheel hubs that are machined from a single block of aluminum are best, but the pressed-metal hubs are considerably less costly. Some prefer hubs with narrow flanges, which make for longer spokes and supposedly a more flexible wheel. The racing fraternity appears to prefer the wide-flange hub.

TIRES

There are four kinds of cycle tires in use today: pneumatics, often simply called tires; balloons; tubulars, also called tubs, sew-ups, or sew-ons; and clinchers, also called wired-ons or wire-ons.

Pneumatics were popular years ago, when they were simply called bicycle tires. Today you find them only on the lower-priced children's cycles and on heavy-duty delivery cycles. They are tough and long-lived. Punctures are easily patched.

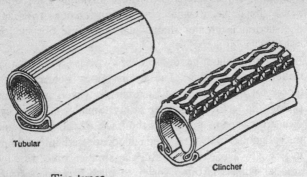

Tubular

Clincher

FIGURE 9. Tire types.

Balloons are heavy-duty workhorse tires. Their cross section is upward of 1 1/2 inches. They are tough, long-lived, and very difficult to pedal, since they are run on low pressure. They are found on the "bomber" type of cycle and on delivery cycles.

Tubulars are first choice for racing and long-distance touring. They are lightest in weight. The "Transalpino Criterium," for example, handmade of silk, weighs only 7 1/2 ounces with its inner tube. A tubular for touring, the Wolber "Renforce," weighs twelve ounces complete with inner tube. Overall cross-section dimension of a tubular is about one inch. Given sufficient care, the heavier sew-ups can go four thousand miles and more before replacement is necessary.

Tubulars are faster than the other tire types, because they are narrower, have less tread on the road, and are normally operated at higher pressure. Over the road the tubular may be filled with eighty pounds of air per square inch (psi). On a hard, indoor track they may be pressurized to 150 psi.

The lightest clinchers weigh 13 1/2 ounces plus the tube, which can go about four or five ounces additional.

48

The more-or-less standard lightweight clincher and tube weigh in well over a pound. The cross-section dimension is 1 1/4 inches minimum, with cross-section thickness of 1 3/8 and 1 3/4 inches available.

Maximum clincher pressure is not much over 85 psi, with 50 or 60 pounds about usual.

Tubulars and clinchers are not interchangeable, although wheel diameters may be the same. Rim cross sections are different. If you are thinking of running two types of tires—one for exercise and one for racing—think of purchasing four wheels to accomplish the change efficiently along with quick-release hubs.

Sew-ups are most costly. The silk tire goes for about sixteen dollars. The heavy-weight cotton tubular fetches about seven dollars. In contrast, a good lightweight clincher such as the Dunlop can be had for seven dollars, and other clincher tires, any size, can be purchased for as little as three dollars.

The sew-ups have lighter, thinner walls, so they are more easily punctured and more quickly worn out than the clinchers. They have less tread on the ground and are harder, so they do not have the traction of clinchers. And if they have natural rubber tubes, they will lose a little air each day and need constant reinflation and attention.

Tubulars are easier to remove from the rim than other tires but are harder and more time-consuming to repair. You can fold them up and carry several under your seat as spares. Actually tubular owners are forced to carry spares, because they are almost impossible to patch in the field. They are called sew-on because the inner tubes are sewn in place with needle and thread. Tubular repair and care require skill and patience.

Should you purchase tubulars, be certain to buy adapters. Tubulars come with European valves—Presta, Woods Continental, and the like. Without an adapter you cannot air them from an American air hose (even with an adapter this must be done with great care, since the tire holds very little air) or an American bicycle pump.

The clincher is similar to an automobile tire. It has a tough outer casing with a wire bead at each edge. Air is held in an inner tube. Like an auto tire, punctures are repaired by sealing the hole in the inner tube with a standard patch similar to that used on an auto tube. We may eventually see tubeless bicycle tires with all the advantages of the tubeless auto tire. But as yet they are not on the scene.

The clincher is heavier, more difficult to puncture, with a longer useful life, and much better wet-weather traction. The clincher is also more difficult to remove. Generally you need tools.

SPEED CHANGERS

The purpose of the speed changer is to vary the gear ratio between your pedals and the rear wheel. A speed changer is a convenience and not a necessity.

There are two kinds of speed changers: hub changers and derailleur-type changers. You can recognize the hub changer by the thickness of the rear-wheel hub and the presence of a little chain coming out of its center. Hub changers normally come in two- and three-speed models. Derailleurs can be recognized by the cluster of five sprockets on the rear hub. To get ten changes two chain wheels are used. To get fifteen changes three chain wheels are necessary.

Gear-in-hub speed changers are to be found on the better general-purpose cycles, rarely on long-distance touring cycles, and never on racers. The sun and planet gear arrangement in the hub speed changers is a less efficient speed changer than the derailleur. The hub changer's advantages lie in its simple configuration; it's easier to keep clean, less likely to be troubled by dirt and the like, and somewhat simpler to operate.

Hub changers are available with back-pedaling brakes. If you want to be doubly secure on stopping, you can fit your wheel with hand brakes and hub brake.

Another point to keep in mind when making a choice between hubs and external gearing is that you can make many of your own repairs on a derailleur. Also, derailleur ratios can be changed. You can change one or more gears on the sprocket cluster, and of course you can change the crank gear or gears. Some crank gears are bolted in place, so the change is relatively simple. Hub changers are complex; their action is out of sight and therefore more difficult to understand and follow.

GEAR RATIO

Cycle literature makes frequent mention of gear ratio, usually in terms incomprehensible to the uninitiated. Typically a figure will be mentioned. It may be 35, 66, 105, or what have you. The faster explanation is the long way around.

Years ago in the days of the Penny Farthing, the pedals were firmly affixed to the front driving wheel. Diameter of these wheels in those days was commonly 60 inches. Every time the cyclist made the pedals go around once, the big wheel rolled about 185 inches or, to be exact, $60 \times \pi$ (3.14). All present-day nomenclature is based on that original 60-inch-diameter wheel, but confusion enters when many biking books imply that the cycle geared to 60 goes 60 inches with each complete turn of the pedals. It doesn't; it goes 185 inches.

Now if your cycle is geared to 60, you are geared

exactly like the old Penny Farthing. If you are geared to 30, you have to rotate your pedals two times to go as far. Geared to 120, you go twice as far, and so on. See Figure 10.

If you recall your high-school physics, you will remember that gearing down increases leverage; thus you want to gear down when you are going uphill.

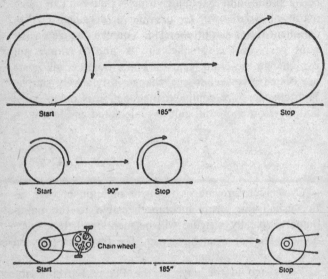

FIGURE 10. How gearing works. The large wheel on top is 60 inches in diameter. Give it one turn, and it rolls about 185 inches. The small wheel is half that diameter. Give it one turn, and it rolls about 92 inches or half the distance covered by the big wheel. Attach a 10-tooth sprocket to the small wheel. Drive it with a 20-tooth chain wheel. Make the chain wheel turn once, and the little wheel will go as far as the big wheel. (The length of the chain has no bearing on the gear ratio.) The ratio of teeth on the chain wheel to the teeth on the little wheel makes the little wheel turn twice for every turn of the chain wheel.

Going downhill and on the flats with a wind behind your back, you want to gear up; you want speed. If you try it, you will find that the gear ratio that lets you pedal up a 10-percent or steeper grade sitting down (it is extremely bad form to stand up and pump) will not permit you to reach thirty miles per hour on the flats or downhill. You will find that you simply cannot move your feet rapidly enough.

The prime reason for gearing is to match your leg power to road conditions. The second reason for gearing is an extension of the first. Each individual has his own best cadence or beat. The difference in pedal-cranking speed from one individual to another varies from 60 crank revolutions per minute to as much as 130 or more. To make the most of your energy, to operate at maximum physical efficiency you need to hold this beat, whatever it is. To change speed you shift gears, but your feet keep rotating at a fixed speed. That is why practiced cyclists appear to be so mechanical to the inexperienced eye.

We can therefore see that you must know what your best pedal speed is; you must get your beat before you can select the gear ratios that suit you best.

FINDING THE RATIO

To find the gear ratios that suit you, borrow or rent a multispeed wheel. Find a flat, smooth road and a windless day. Try several of the middle gears until you find the one with which you can pedal most easily while maintaining a good clip. Obviously the lowest gear will be most easy; the highest most difficult. You have got to find the compromise. A good test might be the highest gear that you can hold steady over thirty minutes or an hour. This then becomes your center gear, and you choose a gear set that gives you a selection of higher and lower speeds.

To find the gear of an existing cycle, divide the number of teeth on the chain wheel by the number of teeth on the rear sprocket. (If you have a hub speed changer, shift to the 1:1 ratio, or no ratio. If you have a derailleur, use the gears the chain is engaging at the moment.) Now multiply the resultant figure by the diameter of the wheel. For example, if the chain wheel has 46 teeth, the rear sprocket has 20 teeth, and the wheel size is 26,

$$\frac{46}{20} \times 26 = 59.8.$$

Using the same chain wheel but shifting the chain to a 23-tooth sprocket produces

$$\frac{46}{23} \times 26 = 52.$$

The easy way is to look it up on Table 1, page 43-44.

CHOOSING RATIOS

The gear ratios you select will vary with your plans and physical condition. Generally, experienced, well-trained cyclists prefer a narrow spread or range of gear ratios. The beginner finds it easier to work with a larger spread of ratios. Perhaps it would be more accurate to say that the soft, out-of-condition cyclist needs the low ratios, whereas the old hand simply never goes down that low, and therefore his gear box would cover a smaller range of ratios with a smaller difference in speed between each step.

TABLE 1. Gear Ratios for Popular 26- and 27-Inch Wheels

NO. OF TEETH ON CHAIN WHEEL

No. of teeth on rear sprocket	24		26		28		30		32		34		36		38		40		42		44	
Wheel size	26 in	27 in	26 in	27 in	26 in	27 in	26 in	27 in	26 in	27 in	26 in	27 in	26 in	27 in	26 in	27 in	26 in	27 in	26 in	27 in	26 in	27 in
12	52.1	54.1	56.3	58.5	60.6	63.0	65.0	67.5	69.2	72.0	73.8	76.5	78.0	81.1	82.4	85.5	86.7	90.0	91.0	94.5	95.3	99.0
13	48.0	49.8	52.0	54.0	56.0	58.1	60.0	62.3	64.1	66.4	68.0	70.6	72.0	74.7	76.0	79.0	80.0	83.1	84.0	87.2	88.0	91.4
14	44.6	46.2	48.2	50.1	52.0	54.0	55.7	57.8	59.5	61.7	63.1	65.5	66.8	69.5	70.6	73.3	74.3	77.1	78.0	81.0	81.7	84.9
15	41.6	43.2	45.0	46.8	48.5	50.4	52.0	54.0	55.5	57.6	59.0	61.1	62.4	64.8	65.9	68.4	69.3	72.0	72.8	75.6	76.3	79.2
16	39.1	40.5	42.2	43.7	45.5	47.2	48.7	50.6	52.0	54.0	55.2	57.2	58.5	60.9	61.8	64.1	65.0	67.5	68.3	70.9	71.5	74.3
17	36.7	38.1	39.7	41.2	42.8	44.4	45.8	47.6	48.9	50.8	52.0	54.0	55.0	57.2	58.1	60.3	61.2	63.5	64.2	66.7	67.3	69.9
18	34.6	36.0	37.5	39.0	40.5	42.0	43.3	45.0	46.2	48.0	49.2	51.0	52.0	54.0	54.9	57.0	57.8	60.0	60.6	63.0	63.6	66.0
19	32.9	34.1	35.5	36.9	38.3	39.7	41.0	42.6	43.8	45.5	46.6	48.2	49.2	51.1	52.0	54.0	54.7	56.8	57.5	59.7	60.2	62.5
20	31.2	32.4	33.8	35.1	36.4	37.8	39.0	40.5	41.6	43.2	44.2	45.9	46.7	48.7	49.4	51.3	52.0	54.0	54.6	56.7	57.2	59.4
21	29.7	30.8	32.1	33.4	34.6	36.1	37.1	38.6	39.7	41.1	42.0	43.7	44.5	46.4	47.1	48.9	49.5	51.4	52.0	54.0	54.5	56.6
22	28.4	29.4	30.7	31.9	33.0	34.3	35.4	36.8	37.9	39.2	40.2	41.6	42.5	44.2	44.9	46.6	47.3	49.1	49.6	51.5	52.0	54.0
23	27.1	28.1	29.3	30.5	31.5	32.8	33.9	35.2	36.2	37.5	38.4	39.8	40.6	42.2	43.0	44.6	45.2	47.0	47.5	49.3	49.8	51.8
24	26.0	27.0	28.1	29.2	30.3	31.5	32.5	33.7	34.7	36.0	36.8	38.2	39.0	40.5	41.2	42.8	43.3	45.0	45.5	47.3	47.7	49.5
25	25.0	25.9	27.0	28.1	29.1	30.2	31.2	32.4	33.3	34.6	35.4	36.7	37.4	38.9	39.5	41.0	41.6	43.2	43.7	45.4	45.8	47.5
26	24.1	24.9	26.0	27.0	28.0	29.0	30.0	31.2	32.0	33.2	34.0	35.3	36.0	37.4	38.0	39.5	40.0	41.5	42.0	43.6	44.0	45.7
28	22.3	23.1	24.1	25.0	26.0	27.0	27.8	28.9	29.7	30.8	31.6	32.8	33.4	34.8	35.3	36.6	37.1	38.6	39.0	40.5	40.9	42.4

NO. OF TEETH ON CHAIN WHEEL

No. of teeth on rear sprocket	45		46		47		48		49		50		52		53		54		55		56	
Wheel size	26 in	27 in	26 in	27 in	26 in	27 in	26 in	27 in	26 in	27 in	26 in	27 in	26 in	27 in	26 in	27 in	26 in	27 in	26 in	27 in	26 in	27 in
12	97.5	101.2	99.7	103.5	101.8	105.7	104.0	108.0	106.1	110.2	108.3	112.5	112.7	117.0	114.8	119.3	117.0	121.5	119.1	123.7	121.3	126.0
13	90.0	93.4	92.0	95.5	94.0	97.6	96.0	99.7	98.0	101.8	100.0	103.9	104.0	108.0	106.0	110.0	108.0	112.1	110.0	114.2	112.0	116.3
14	83.5	86.7	85.4	88.7	87.2	90.6	89.1	92.6	90.9	94.5	92.9	96.4	96.6	100.3	98.4	102.2	100.3	104.1	102.1	106.0	104.0	108.0
15	78.0	80.9	79.7	82.8	81.5	84.6	83.2	86.4	84.9	88.2	86.7	90.0	90.1	93.6	91.8	95.4	93.6	97.2	95.3	99.0	97.1	100.8
16	73.1	76.0	74.6	77.8	76.3	79.3	78.0	81.0	79.6	82.7	81.3	84.4	84.5	87.8	86.1	89.4	87.5	91.1	89.3	92.8	91.0	94.5
17	68.8	71.5	70.4	73.1	71.9	74.6	73.4	76.2	74.9	77.8	76.5	79.4	79.5	82.6	81.0	84.1	82.6	85.7	84.1	87.3	85.8	88.9
18	65.0	67.5	66.4	69.0	67.9	70.5	69.3	72.0	70.7	73.5	72.2	75.0	75.1	78.0	76.5	79.5	78.0	81.0	79.4	82.5	80.8	84.0
19	61.7	64.0	62.9	65.4	64.3	66.8	65.7	68.2	67.0	69.6	68.4	71.1	71.1	73.9	72.5	75.3	73.9	76.7	75.2	78.1	76.6	79.5
20	58.5	60.8	59.8	62.1	61.1	63.5	62.4	64.8	63.6	66.2	65.0	67.5	67.6	70.2	68.9	71.5	70.2	72.9	71.5	74.6	72.8	75.6
21	55.8	57.9	57.0	59.1	58.2	60.4	59.4	61.7	60.6	63.0	61.9	64.3	64.4	66.9	65.6	68.1	66.9	69.4	68.1	70.7	69.3	72.0
22	53.1	55.3	54.4	56.5	55.5	57.6	56.7	58.9	57.8	60.1	59.1	61.4	61.5	63.8	62.6	65.0	63.8	66.2	65.0	67.5	66.1	68.7
23	50.9	52.8	52.0	54.0	53.1	55.1	54.3	56.3	55.4	57.5	56.5	58.7	58.8	61.1	59.9	62.2	61.0	63.5	62.1	64.5	63.3	65.7
24	48.6	50.6	49.9	51.8	50.9	52.9	51.9	54.0	53.1	55.1	54.2	56.3	56.3	58.5	57.4	59.6	58.5	60.7	59.5	61.8	60.6	63.0
25	46.9	48.6	47.8	49.7	48.9	50.8	49.9	51.9	51.0	53.0	52.0	54.0	54.1	56.2	55.1	57.2	56.1	58.3	57.2	59.4	58.2	60.4
26	45.0	46.7	46.0	47.8	47.0	48.8	48.0	49.9	49.0	50.9	50.0	51.9	52.0	54.0	53.0	55.1	54.0	56.0	55.0	57.1	56.0	58.1
28	41.8	43.4	42.7	44.4	43.6	45.3	44.6	46.3	45.5	47.2	46.4	48.2	48.3	50.1	49.2	51.1	50.1	52.0	51.0	53.0	52.0	54.0

In any event, the beginner is advised to try the gear ratios he selects, if he can, before he commits himself to purchase. Let's assume you can somehow manage to get the ante up and are planning to purchase a cycle with more than one gear ratio. What ratios should you select?

If you are the typical weekend cycler, you will want lower ratio gearing. If you are a seasoned pro, you will want your gears closer to the top. Generally it is not wise to select as wide a spread of ratios as the machine will bear. You do not get an all-out spread on the hub changers, and only the better derailleurs will handle more than a limited spread.

Should you spend most or all of your time on the flats, there is little point in fitting a very low ratio to the bike. If you are, on the other hand, planning to challenge the Rockies, with full panniers weighing forty or fifty pounds, you will naturally seek lower gearing. There is no sense in fitting a gear ratio to the bike which will permit you to go twenty-two miles per hour when you know you won't need it in hill country.

For the average weekend cyclist, the ratios shown in Table 2 are suggested.

The ratios in Table 2 have been selected with somewhat hilly country in mind. If you live in the Midwest or similar more-or-less level areas, you may want to push your range up a bit.

There is of course little chance that any of the gears available will work out as evenly as the numbers listed. They are merely guides. You will encounter ratios such as 38.6, 96.4, and so on. This is to be expected and will be close enough. Just for the record, 60 is considered normal for the average rider.

TABLE 2. *Suggested Gear Ratios*

2-SPEED	3-SPEED	5-SPEED	10-SPEED	15-SPEED
52	48	46	44	38
70	60	64	48	42
	78	70	52	46
		78	56	50
			60	54
			64	58
			68	62
			72	68
			76	72
			80	76
				80
				84
				88
				92
				96

HANDLEBARS

If you are just going around the corner, you will probably want a flat or upright handlebar. If you plan to cycle a mite more, you will want a racing-type or dropped handlebar. There are many types, but all may be classified as variations on a basic theme: a downward curve. Some of the more famous designs include the Maes, Capo Berta, Pista, and Randonneur. The Randonneur is most often selected for touring, because its flat section offers a greater choice of hand positions. The Pista is one of the more curved designs.

Don't invest in high-rise handlebars. They look like giant V's, and you ride as though someone had a gun at your back. They are difficult to manage, awkward

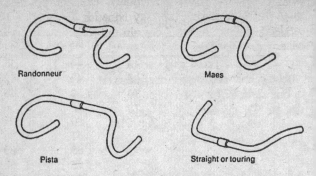

Randonneur

Maes

Pista

Straight or touring

FIGURE 11. Some of the better-known handlebar designs.

when mounting or dismounting; in short, they are a pain and dangerous to boot. To be comfortable while cycling for any length of time your arms must be more or less parallel. To control your front wheel well you need your hands where you can swing them. In a sitting position this is about hip height, which places your hands, when you're in the saddle and leaning forward comfortably, just about the height of the saddle.

Be certain to plug the ends of your handlebars. Use the rubber grips, or use the expanding plugs sold for this purpose. The edges of the handlebars are sharp, and you can gash yourself quite badly on them should you spill.

HANDLEBAR EXTENSIONS

This fitment was invented by champion racer Major Taylor, and his device is often referred to as a Taylor outrigger. It enables the cyclist to lean as far forward as he wishes or as he may need to do because of his arm length. Major Taylor, incidentally, chalked up many racing records during the Gay Nineties. Three that he established back in 1891 remain unbroken to this date by anyone on either side of the Atlantic. Major Taylor usually rode a fixed gear of 92.

Handlebar stems and extensions are most often made in one stem length, which is usually five inches, and two designs. One design has a clamp arrangement on the extension which permits the cyclist to adjust and set his handlebars any distance he wishes, from almost zero to perhaps five inches ahead. The other design comes with a fixed extension and a choice of extension lengths ranging from about 1 3/4 inches to 4 inches. The fixed-extension design stem is lighter and somewhat prettier. Both types may be seen in Figure 12.

This handlebar stem is adjustable.

The vertical stem of this design is 5½ inches long. The extension length can be had in five sizes, ranging from 1¾ to 4 inches.

FIGURE 12. Examples of handlebar stems.

One changes extensions or adjusts handlebar setting to accommodate one's reach. If the present stem on your cycle does not permit you to satisfy your reach, try moving the seat forward or backward as the need may be. This may save you the cost of a new stem.

Two types of brakes are in use today: (1) hand brakes, sometimes called caliper brakes, and (2) coaster brakes or foot brakes. The first type is controlled by levers attached to the handlebars, one lever for the front wheel and another for the rear wheel. The coaster brake is controlled or operated by pedaling backward.

The coaster brake is identified by the thick rear hub and a short flat lever extending from the hub to a clip attached to a chain stay. It is found on the lower-cost cycle and sometimes is incorporated into a speed-changer hub. The coaster-brake mechanism is out of sight and needs no adjustment or attention beyond oiling. Repairing a coaster brake is usually complicated and best left to an expert.

In operation the coaster brake is very effective because the cyclist leans back when he applies reverse pedal pressure, thus placing much of his weight where it is needed at the time—at the rear wheel. Because one pedals backward to stop, it is an easy brake for beginners.

The hand brake requires a little more experience, but the hand brake when properly adjusted has absolutely no drag on the wheel. (Coaster brakes always drag a bit on the wheel.)

Hand-brake shoes wear, and they require periodic adjustment. However, since the brake itself is highly visible and simple, inspection and adjustment involve only a minute's work. So far as braking efficiency is concerned, both types stop equally well on dry surfaces. The hand brakes are more efficient on wet and slippery surfaces because both wheels take hold. Another point in favor of hand brakes: There are two of them, and they are independent. You can lose one and still get home.

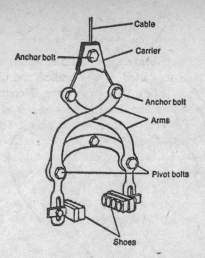

FIGURE 13. Center-pull caliper brake.

There are two types of hand brakes: center pull and side pull. The major advantage of the center pull is that it can wobble to some extent with the wheel. This is not a condition that should be long tolerated, but the ability of the center-pull brake to swing from side to side with a crooked wheel can help one get home without walking.

SEATS

Some people like fat, stubby seats. Racers usually select long, narrow seats, and tour cyclists usually select a compromise design.

If you can finance it, purchase a leather seat. Leather absorbs moisture, whereas the plastic seat does not. Leather has some natural resiliency and with time will

61

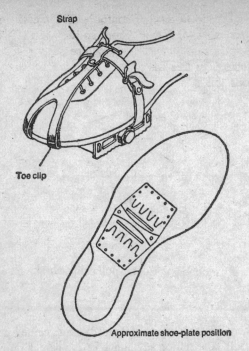

Strap

Toe clip

Approximate shoe-plate position

FIGURE 14. Toe clip and strap. Shoe plate fastened to bottom of shoe keeps foot from moving backward.

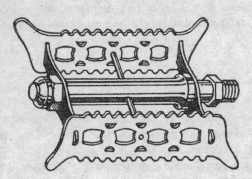

FIGURE 15. Standard Milremo rat-trap pedal.

give and conform to your contours. The plastic remains hard and unyielding throughout its life span.

There is also considerable choice in springing and cushioning. In this matter you can let your conscience be your guide.

PEDALS

The all-metal pedal, most commonly referred to as the rat trap, is far superior to the conventional rubber pedal. The rubber pedals are heavier and slippery when wet.

Rat traps come in a variety of designs. Some have reflectors on their sides, some have toe clips and straps. You will find that you need cycle shoes with rat traps. If you wear sneakers and pedal rat traps for any length of time, you will imagine your feet are being cut in two. Ordinary shoes are fine for short jaunts, but their stiffness and weight add to the pedaling load.

Bike racing shoes are light and highly flexible, but they should be fitted with cleats. These are metal pads that screw on to the bottom of the shoe and fit into the rat trap, preventing your foot from moving forward or backward when the slot in the cleat engages the pedal. When positioning the cleat, leave a breath of space between the toe of your shoe and the inside of the toe clip. If you don't, there will be continuous pressure on your toes, and eventually discomfort.

LIGHTS

There are battery-powered lights and generator-powered lights. My vote is in favor of battery lights. True, you never forget to replace the old batteries when you have a generator, and the generator never runs down. But the generator produces power only when you are moving. The light goes out when you stop, and there will be times when you will need to walk your cycle and when you need the light for purposes other than illuminating yourself and the road ahead. In addition, generators drag and add an extra load on the cyclist and also tend to wear the tire a bit.

If you do use battery-powered lights, you must remember to replace old cells. Use the cadmium cells; they cost more but last much longer.

Whether or not you plan to cycle at night, be certain to install a large reflector on the rear of your wheel. This will be of some help if some unforeseen circumstance should keep you out after nightfall. If you do plan to cycle at night, mount a second light, a red one, on the rear of your cycle. Some state laws require you to have a white light up front which must be visible for some five hundred feet. This is fine, but it is more important that you be seen from the rear, so get a second light for the rear. Also, it is an excellent idea to purchase the new pedals with reflectors on their sides.

CHAPTER 5

Care

All a bike asks is to be brought in out of the rain, wiped dry when wet, lubricated, and tightened up once in a while. If you provide your cycle with this minimum of attention, you will be rewarded with many thousand trouble-free miles.

This statement will now be followed by several hundred well-chosen words and illustrations detailing bike care and repair.

Which way do you jump?

If you are a Sunday cyclist and you give your wheel a minimum of attention and care, you may expect to run maybe three to four years without trouble.

If you cycle more than a few hours a week, if you really roll up the miles and you want your wheel in peak condition, if you want to pass it on to your son and he to your grandson (and it can be done)—a kiss and a promise will not suffice.

If your plans for your cycle and your riding habit fall somewhere between these two extremes, tailor your bike-care program to suit.

EXTERNAL CARE

If you want to keep your bike bright and shiny, *don't wipe it down.* The dust that collects contains abrasive particles that produce fine scratches on the paint and bare metal when removed by wiping. This is true even though you use a very clean, soft cloth each time you wipe. Instead wash your cycle with clean lukewarm water—no soap—and then wipe it dry.

To reduce mud and soil adhesion it is advisable to wax your cycle's painted and nickel-plated or chromium-plated surfaces. There are hundreds of waxes on the market. You can use any wax you wish, provided it is not a "cleaner." This may sound like an impossible choice, since almost all waxes and polishes are marked "cleaner." To a certain extent every wax is a cleaner since it will remove dirt. However, we want "pure" wax without abrasive and chemical cleaners. If the label doesn't say "cleaner," your problem is solved. If it does, test it by rubbing the wax on a painted surface and then rubbing it off. If some of the paint comes off in the form of "color" on the cloth, the polish or wax contains a cleaner. Do not use it to wax your cycle.

We now have the correct wax on hand. What to do? Wash the cycle down with warm water and a little detergent. Don't use regular soap, because it leaves a film. Wipe dry, and apply the wax; rub it in. Don't worry about getting a little wax into the cracks or into the bearings. It will do no harm unless you actually force wax inside, and this is very difficult to do. Don't fret about getting too much wax on or not rubbing hard enough or long enough. If the wheel shines, you have rubbed hard enough.

Wax does several things. It sort of waterproofs the metal, making the water run off quickly. It reduces the adherence of dirt and soil, and it reduces the bleaching and drying action of the sun on the paint.

The reason the wheel is not washed with soap and water each time it gets dirty, but only with plain water, is that the soap removes the wax. When the wax has been on a couple of months, you can remove the wax with soap and water or simply add more wax.

If the paint and/or metal has faded on your cycle and you want to improve its appearance, use a "cutting" agent to remove the top layer of faded paint. There are several good, fine-abrasive mixtures on the market compounded for just this purpose. They are generally called cleaners. Two good ones that come to mind are Green Turtle and Simonize. Green Turtle comes in two grades; use the finer (less coarse) grade.

To use, wash the frame down with soap and water, dry, and apply a daub of the cleaner to a portion of the frame. Rub that area until the paint gets bright or until you no longer hear the scouring, cutting action of the cleaner. Then add more cleaner, and use a fresh, clean section of your cloth. You will know that you are removing paint because you will see the paint on your rag. Keep using fresh cleaner and fresh rags until the entire frame is bright. Make certain that you have not overlooked any areas and that there are no "lines" between areas that are darker or lighter than the rest. This done, wash the remains of the cleaner off with warm soap and water, and wax.

If the paint is really faded and you cannot reach bright color, or if someone has botched the frame up with house paint or something, repaint the entire frame. (See Chapter 15, under "Repainting.")

You should make it a practice to check your equipment before you ride off in the morning and again after you have ridden for several hours and have stopped. Inspection should not take more than a few minutes and will save you the embarrassment and worse that may occur should you break down on the road. Periodic inspections will also greatly prolong the life of your wheel.

The following should be included in your check-out schedule. The order is unimportant, but you will be less likely to overlook any steps if you establish a pattern and stick with it.

Examine the surface of the tires. Look for pieces of glass, nails, and so on. Remove.

Squeeze the tires. They should be so hard they do not give. If you can compress the tire with your fingers, it needs air. If you have recently aired it, it is leaking. Find leak and repair. (See Chapter 7, on tires.)

Inspect the air-valve stem. It should be pointing directly toward the center of the wheel. If it is tilted, the tire is loose on the rim and has shifted. Correct.

Push the front wheel sideways toward the frame. A machined hub will allow no play. Pressed hubs allow a barely perceptible play. If side play is clearly evident, the bearing cones are loose. Correct. Do the same with the rear wheel. (See Chapter 8, on wheels.)

Listen to the ratchet. Raise the rear wheel by placing your hand under the seat. Spin the wheel forward. The clicking sound should be smooth. The wheel should make many turns before stopping.

Check for wheel rub. Lift the rear wheel, spin wheel; listen for rub. Repeat with the front wheel. Wheels should make several turns before stopping.

Test hand brakes. Squeeze each brake in turn about twice as hard as you would in an emergency stop. If the cable is weak, you want it to give way now. (See Chapter 9, on brakes.)

Test the coaster brake. Ride the cycle; try an emergency stop. You should be able to make the wheel skid.

Check the pedal crank arm for play. Push the pedal toward the bike frame and then away from the bike frame. There should be no play. If loose, tighten. (See Chapter 10, on pedals and cranks.)

Check the pedals. Hold the pedal crank arm firm with one hand. Lift and lower the pedal. There should be very little play. If loose, tighten. Spin pedals. They should rotate freely for a considerable length of time. If not, they probably need lubrication or new bearings. Correct.

Check the chain. Place your hand on the chain about halfway between the chain wheel and the rear sprocket. Lift. If there is more than a half-inch of play, it is loose. Tighten, but leave at least a quarter-inch on vertical freedom. (See Figure 16 and Chapter 11, on chains and chain wheels.)

Check the derailleur gear position. This is something you should do every time you leave the cycle unattended in a public place. Kids—adults too—have itchy fingers. If they move the front and/or rear derailleur lever and you pedal off in your normal zippy style, there is a good chance the chain will either damage a gear or slip off the gears altogether. Either lift the rear of the cycle and turn the crank slowly with your hand, once or twice, or pedal very slowly, while sitting the bike, until the chain slips into its proper place. Afterward you can shift to the gear of your choice.

Check the derailleur action. Watch the chain as you shift it from one gear to another. It should not rub on any gear; it should not touch the wheel spokes or chain stays. If the chain does, correct before riding further, or damage will result. (See Chapter 12, on derailleurs.)

Check the handlebars. Lock the front wheel between your knees. You should not be able to turn the handlebars without exerting considerable force. You want them tight but not "locked." Should you spill, it is best that the handlebars turn and give a bit. Adjust the stem bolt as necessary. Put your weight on the ends of the handlebars. If the bars tilt down, you need to tighten the clamping bolt. Now lift the cycle up by the

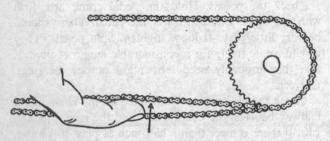

FIGURE 16. Simple chain-slack test. Lift lower section of chain in center portion of arc. Estimate or measure distance chain can be lifted.

Minimum: ¼ inch. All chains, all positions.

Maximum: ½ inch. Derailleur chains on largest chain wheel and largest rear sprocket. All nonderailleur chains.

1 inch. Derailleur chains on smallest chain wheel and smallest rear sprocket.

handlebars and lower quickly. This should uncover any looseness present in the head set. (See Chapter 14, on head sets, handlebars, and seats.)

Check the seat. Push down on the rear edge with one hand, and pull up on the front of the seat with the other. If you can tilt the seat, it is loose. Correct.

All cycles may be properly lubricated with just two types of grease and one type of oil. How and when you apply lubricants to your bicycle depends on how often and how far you ride, the type of cycle you own, and how long you want it to last.

All cycles (except multiseaters) have six ball-bearing assemblies: the head set, the crank hanger, the two wheel hubs, and the two pedals. The ball-bearing assemblies rely *primarily* on grease for lubrication. The grease may or may not be supplemented by oil, as shall be explained. All other moving parts are lubricated by oil alone.

Oil is our best lubricant. However, ball bearings will not retain oil without a seal. Cycle bearings are not sealed. One reason might be the additional weight and size of bearing seals. Another is that a seal rubs on the shaft (thus sealing the oil), and the advantage of oil might be lost to the increased friction of the seal. Grease is the lubricant used, therefore.

The parts of precision-made wheel hubs and chainwheel hangers fit so perfectly that little grease escapes. These bearing assemblies are not oiled and have no provisions for adding oil. The hubs and hangers of less carefully made wheels and cranks do leak grease. These components have holes leading to their innards. When a hub or crank hanger is fitted with an oil cup, you oil it. Figure 17 shows some typical oil cups and covers. When the hubs and crank have no opening for oiling, you don't oil it.

The head-set bearing assembly is never oiled. This is true of both the expensive and the less expensive machines. The pedal bearings on all bikes are always both greased and oiled.

Why grease and oil? The precision hubs and hangers

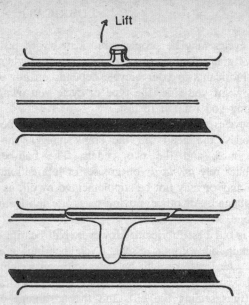

FIGURE 17. Two types of oil holes and covers. The one on top is called an oil cup; you lift its cover off. The one on the bottom is rotated or slid to one side.

leak grease very slowly, so slowly that with ordinary riding you can keep them properly lubricated by regreasing once or twice a year. The pressed hubs and some crank hangers lose grease very rapidly, simply because there is more space between the parts. To keep these hubs properly lubricated it would be necessary to grease them perhaps six or more times a year. Since greasing requires the component to be disassembled, cleaned, and reassembled, cyclists are naturally loath to spend the time. Oil is therefore introduced into the assembly behind the bearings. The oil mixes with the remaining grease and completes the seal. In time, however, the now thinned grease will run out. When this happens, there is nothing between the balls to stop the flow of oil. Added oil runs out very quickly. Therefore it is necessary to repack the bearings with grease every so often. As can be seen, adding oil is merely a gimmick to reduce the number of times the low-quality assemblies have to be regreased.

You can run the wheel on oil alone, but it will be awfully messy, and there are no data on how long the oil will remain inside and lubricate. When you hear a squeak, it's too late.

LUBRICANTS

Since the oil we squirt into the hubs and other parts tends to run out through the spaces between the moving parts, it behooves us to use a rather heavy oil. The high-priced, high-detergency, 10-20-30 W oil sold for use in cars is not the one you want. Purchase the low-price SAE 30 oil—the oil that comes in cans that read "pure" Pennsylvania, California, or what have you. The high-priced oil is only one-half oil; the other half is a mixture of cleaners, rust preventatives, anti-frothing agents, and the like—fine for cars but not for cycles.

We use grease to seal the spaces between the ball bearings, and we want the grease to have body. But overly heavy grease will not do. When thick grease is pushed aside, it remains aside, and when the grease is too thick, it is quite possible for the ball bearings to run around in a "dry" groove within the grease. It is not until heat is generated by friction that the grease melts and starts lubricating under such circumstances.

We therefore apply a light grease such as Gold Seal, Lubriplate Type A, Molykote G, GI (government-issued) OG-OO, or a lightweight automotive front-wheel bearing grease if nothing else is available. Some cyclists are wary of Molykote G on the free-wheel bear-

73

ings and pawl and suggest a lightweight oil instead. Some suggest a light coat of "Moly" when you are assembling dissimilar metals, which you will be doing should you have a steel crank axle and duraluminum crank arms. The Moly supposedly prevents corrosion from forming between the two metals and "locking" the pieces together.

If you have been following all this carefully, you will recall that a third lubricant was mentioned. We need a slightly heavier grease for the head set. The shaft here is in a vertical position, and we need a more tenacious grease. We can use the aforementioned auto grease, Lubriplate Low Temp or Starfak No. 2. Suitable grease and oil can be purchased from your local cycle shop or one of the mail-order houses listed at the end of the book.

LUBRICATION EQUIPMENT

All you really need is a pressure oiler, which you can buy for a couple of dollars. When you use it, limit yourself to one squirt per hub. Don't force so much oil in that you force the grease out. Something between a half and one teaspoon is about right.

You will want some clean paper cups for parts and a large metal or plastic dish for the cleaning fluid. Getting rid of the fluid is a problem. Don't dump it down the kitchen sink. The sewer in front of the house isn't bad, but the safest place is a corner of the back yard where nothing is growing. The gas or kerosine will soak into the earth and will eventually be destroyed by bacteria.

LUBRICATION SCHEDULE

It is good practice to lubricate a new cycle before you take it out for its first ride. This is especially valid advice for a low- to medium-priced cycle. Some of these wheels remain in the warehouse a long time. The grease dries out. Top-grade wheels are assembled on order, or you may actually put the parts together yourself, so there is little chance of these parts running dry.

Assuming that the cycle is freshly cleaned and lubricated, see Table 3 for a cleaning and lubrication schedule designed for the average rider.

TABLE 3. *Cleaning and Lubrication Schedule*

Head set	1/year	Clean and grease
Crank hanger	2/year	Clean and grease
	1/month	Oil, if possible
Front hub	2/year	Clean and grease
	1/200 mi.	Oil
Rear hub	2/year	Clean and grease
	1/200 mi.	Oil
Chain	4/year	Clean and oil
	1/100 mi.	Oil
	After rain	Oil
Pedals	2/year	Clean and grease
	1/100 mi.	Oil
Brakes (hand)	3/year	Oil
Coaster brake	1/year	Clean and grease
	2/year	Oil
Hub gears	1/year	Clean and grease
	2/year	Oil
Derailleur	2/year	Clean and grease
	1/100 mi.	Oil
Free wheel	2/year	Clean and oil
	1/200 mi.	Oil

LUBRICATION PROCEDURE

The actual steps necessary to remove, disassemble, and replace the various components that require lubrication are discussed in later chapters. These paragraphs are concerned with lubrication only.

Before you begin taking your cycle apart, spend a few minutes cleaning it. This will lessen the chance of dirt entering any of the bearing assemblies. Also provide yourself with a clean working area that won't be harmed by grease and oil. A heavy layer of newspapers will do.

BEARING MECHANISMS

When taking the ball-bearing mechanisms apart try to keep count of the bearings that come out of each race. This will simplify their return.

Your next step will be cleaning the parts. Most of the old timers prefer kerosine for cleaning. Some even warn against using gasoline. Kerosine is thinner than gasoline and will pass through a crack that will hold gas. Thus kerosine is probably a better cleaning agent than gas. However, kerosine dries very slowly, whereas gas evaporates quickly. Both fluids are cutting agents; they have no lubricating properties whatsoever. If all the kerosine is not removed, it may dilute the lubricant, or it may exclude the lubricant. In the latter case the part may run "dry" at that point, and wear will be rapid.

Gasoline, of course, requires care. Its fumes tend to spread over the ground and are easily ignited.

The parts to be cleaned are placed in a container with the cleaning fluid and brushed vigorously. When all the dirt has been removed, the parts are drained and washed in a second container filled with the clean fluid.

You cannot get parts clean in dirty fluid. Then the parts are shaken and blotted dry with a clean cloth.

After all the parts have been thoroughly cleaned and dried, examine the ball bearings and their cones and races carefully. The bearings should be shiny and smooth. If they are discolored, rough, or chewed, they must be replaced. If the bearings are rough, the cones and the races in which the bearings roll around are also most likely worn. You will see alternate shiny and dark spots or a rough surface and scratches when the cones and races are damaged. Generally, when this is the case, it is best to replace the entire unit. There is no point to installing new bearings and new cones when the races are defective. The rough races will damage the bearings, which will quickly damage the cone. In addition, pedaling will be more difficult.

To make certain you secure the correct new replacement bearings when you do not know the make and model number of your hub or hanger, bring the old bearings to the cycle shop. Purchase a few extra; you may need them.

Be certain to use bearings of the correct size. If the bearings are too large, there will be too much clearance between the cone and race, and the grease will leak out very quickly. If the bearings are too small, the cone will rub on the race edge instead of rolling smoothly.

To replace the bearings, line the race with a thin layer of grease and place the bearings in position. If you know the count, you have no problem. If you lost track, keep adding bearings until you have a complete circle, each bearing being placed a little distance from its neighbor. The easy way is to add bearings until one won't go in all the way. When you remove this one, the bearings will appear too loose, but this is the correct spacing. After the bearings have been positioned, add another layer of grease.

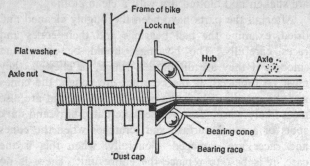

FIGURE 18. Basic bearing arrangement used on all moving parts. The component shown is a wheel hub.

All bearings aren't loose in their races. You will find some in retainer rings—little circular cages that hold the bearings in position and make life lots easier. When cleaning these, take the time necessary to get all the old grease out. When adding new grease, use your fingers to force the grease inside. The retainers go back with the flat side out—toward the end of the axle. If you wish, try them without grease to be certain you have them right, then grease and assemble.

Loose or caged, you will want to cover the bearings with about a quarter of an inch of grease and perhaps twice this thickness of grease in the crank hanger. You don't want the hub loaded with grease, though it might appear to be a good idea. The reason for not doing this is the nature of grease itself. Grease will not move until it has been warmed. So a hub full of grease will only block the flow of oil that you may add later on.

CHAINS

Chains require somewhat special treatment. They must be removed and then cleaned by soaking and scrubbing in kerosine or gasoline. Afterward the chain is generally soaked in lubricating oil. Some cyclists suggest the chain be soaked in very hot, heavy oil, SAE 90, which is actually a grease. Others soak the chain in comparatively light oil and then rub it with a graphite grease combination, which can be purchased in stick form at auto supply houses and cycle shops. This writer recommends that the cleaned chain be soaked in SAE 30 oil and that the chain be worked and rapped while under oil to remove entrapped air.

After the chain has been lubricated, it is lightly wiped with a clean cloth. You want a little lube on the outside of the chain to reduce chain-wheel and sprocket wear. On the other hand, grease and oil hold grit, which increases wear. There is no real answer as to how much lube you leave on the outside of the chain, since you are wrong no matter what you do—the chain and gear teeth will wear. We just make the best of it.

DERAILLEURS

The assembly holding the control lever or levers is not lubricated. These levers are moved so infrequently, in comparison to the rest of the derailleur mechanism, that they suffer no wear. A lubricant on the friction plates will make the control levers slip. A bit of grease should be spread over the control cables at the point where they enter the tubes.

The springs, moving parts of the parallelogram,

control levers, and other moving parts should be given a drop of oil about once a month. The oil is applied at the joints (pivots).

The idler and tension wheels—the two little rascals that ride on the chain—should be taken down, cleaned, and their innards greased every six months. Do this more often if you have been riding the back trails. Watch the bearings in the idler and tension wheels; don't lose any.

The free wheel should be removed and cleaned by soaking in kerosine or gasoline every six months. Grease is not recommended, because it can hold the pawls away from the cog when it is thick with cold or dirt. When this happens, you will pedal without moving. Use an oil. Some cyclists prefer an oil as light as SAE 5, in place of the pure SAE 30 that this writer recommends for all bike lubrication points needing oil. The free wheel can be oiled by removing the wheel and placing it free-wheel side up. Pour some oil into the joint between the free-wheel center and its external hub; let it soak overnight. Wipe the remaining oil off. You can lay some cycles on their sides and squirt the oil into the free-wheel joint.

PEDALS

Pedals should be taken down, cleaned, and greased with light grease about twice a year. Pedals carry a heavy load, since there are many times when the cyclist places all his weight on one foot and then pushes down. Pedals also are very close to the ground and subjected to considerable dirt and water. Between greasings the pedals should be lubricated with oil, about once every hundred miles.

A few drops of oil are applied to the center bolts holding the caliper arms, and a few drops to the steel spring to keep it from rusting. The cable should be greased before it is inserted into its tube. Once in place the exposed sections of the cable should be given a light coating of grease when you think of it. To lubricate a cable already in its tube, disconnect the hand lever, lift it up as high as it can go, and then direct a few drops of oil inside the tube. Give the oil enough time to run down before reassembling. Also put a few drops of oil on the hand-lever pivots.

Coaster brakes are lubricated by squirting some oil into the coaster-brake hub. About one squirt, a teaspoon or so, twice a year will do it. Use SAE 30 oil.

So far we have discussed "running" parts which need lubrication to prevent galling and wear. Other parts of the cycle that do not actually run also need a bit of oil now and again to prevent rust. These parts include all steel nuts and bolts, the axle of the little wheel that carries the speed changer cable, the adjustment nut and ferrule on the brake cables, and so on. The oil is applied, permitted to stand a few minutes, and then wiped off. This will not prevent rusting but will reduce the rust and make it easy to loosen the parts when you want to.

ANTITHEFT SUGGESTIONS

There is an ancient saying that locks are made to keep honest people out. It's still quite valid. Nothing short of an armed guard or a giant safe deposit box will protect your wheel from someone determined to steal it. But even a four-hundred-dollar bike isn't worth this much effort. However, even the least expensive bike is worth the trouble of getting on and riding away.

Therefore don't make the mistake of encouraging crime by leaving your wheel unlocked and unattended. If you lock it properly and securely, very few individuals will even consider stealing it.

Get a good, strong chain made expressly for the purpose, one that cannot be cut with a cable cutter. Fit it with a length of rubber or plastic hose to protect the paint, and get a good pin-tumbler lock, the kind that cannot be broken or easily picked.

Lead the chain through a wheel, through the center of the frame, and then around or through an iron fence or street light pole. Don't just lock the bike to itself. It is too easy to cart away. If possible, chain your bike up in a public place, so that criminals intent on cutting the chain or picking the lock must work out in the open. And move it at least once a day, or it will go, despite the best lock and chain.

You will find the serial number on the underside of the crank hanger, the top of the seat post, and the end of the rear stays. Records yours; you may need it should your bike be stolen and become subject to controversy.

STORAGE

If you have the space, you can store your cycle by simply standing it up with the aid of its stand. An old bed sheet or tablecloth will serve as a dust cover. If you are storing the cycle iin a damp basement or similar place, rub a little oil on all the steel nuts and bolts, and a little on the spokes if they are also of steel.

You can hang your cycle from the rafters by ropes, which for convenience can be fitted with rubber-covered hooks. Or you can drive large nails into a rafter, cover the nails with lengths of rubber hose, and hang your cycle that way. This clears the floor somewhat and gets the cycle out from underfoot. As far as saving the tires is concerned, you'll be hard pressed to notice the difference in life span between tires (other than natural rubber) that have stood on the ground all winter and tires that have been suspended in air.

When space is a problem, disassemble the machine. Place the chain and a few drops of oil in a plastic bag. Seal it. Place the wheels in the large plastic bags used for collecting leaves. This will keep oil drom dripping on the floor. Wipe the chain wheel dry, and wrap a plastic bag around it to keep its drips from the floor. Slip the handlebars out of their clamp. Now you can fit the parts into a package, one that will easily fit into a closet.

Most cycle repairs and part replacements are minor bits of surgery that can be accomplished by anyone taking the trouble to think a little. The same minor repairs are expensive in terms of time lost, nuisance, and actual dollars when they are accomplished at the bike shop. The wheel has to be brought to the shop, left there, picked up, and paid for. There are other good reasons for doing the repairs yourself. Primarily, I think, is the pleasure and satisfaction of working with things you love, be it a cycle, a garden, or a home. Perhaps just as important is the feeling of self-sufficiency mechanical knowledge of your cycle will give you. In the field, knowledge and experience can prove invaluable. With only a few tools, easily transported in a bag beneath your seat, you can cope with most cycle-breakdown emergencies. This makes you free to roam at will. The danger of having to walk home from a hundred-mile cycle ride is virtually eliminated, as is the alternative of phoning a noncycling friend with a car, which can be almost as painful.

TOOLS

You don't need a complex arsenal of equipment, but you do need some tools, and these must be the correct tools or you will find yourself expending considerable needless effort. There are inexpensive tools. Depending on your cycle and what you plan to do, you can probably outfit yourself fairly completely for less than ten dollars. One trip to the bike shop can run more than that.

You will need slim, open-end wrenches—spanners, the English call them—for working on the bearing cones on the front and rear wheels (assuming you do not have quick-release hubs) and for working on the pedals. You will need one large open-end wrench for the nut on the crank assembly and another for the large nut atop the head set. Depending on the design of your crank hanger, you may also need a C spanner and a slot wrench. If you have a cotterless crank, you will need a special removal tool. (See Chapter 10, on pedals and cranks, for details.)

In addition, you will need a hand-operated air pump, a tire pressure gauge, a spoke wrench that fits your spokes, a pressure oil can, and a pair of tire irons (for clinchers only).

All the tools listed above may be termed special tools, since it is not likely that you own them already. To some extent you can make do with a very large crescent wrench or a monkey or Stillson wrench for the large nuts. Wrap the part with adhesive tape before using the Stillson, since it will chew up the metal otherwise. You can sometimes use a screwdriver and ham-

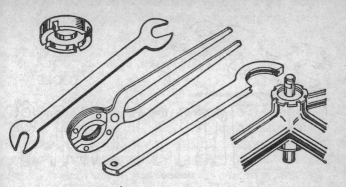

FIGURE 19. Left to right: spoke nipple key, pedal spanner, steering head pliers, and C spanner.

FIGURE 20. Left: Bottom bracket bearing wrench.
Right: Cotterless crank extractor.

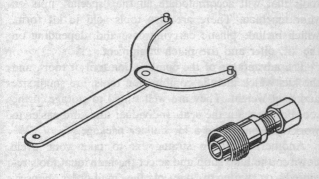

mer to work on a slotted nut. However, if the nut is frozen (rusted tight), you may ruin the nut without loosening it. You will encounter the same difficulty with pliers; if the nuts are frozen, you will round them off without turning them.

A cycle has several different-sized nuts. You can purchase several different wrenches, which will be most ex-

87

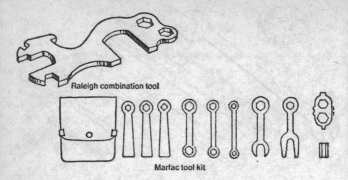

Raleigh combination tool

Marfac tool kit

FIGURE 21. Combination tool and tool kit.

pensive but most convenient for working, or you can, if you are lucky, purchase one, two, or three combination tools that will accommodate all the "special" nuts on your machine. There are also tools sold in kit form, which include plastic carrying case and, depending on the kit, oiler and tire patch equipment.

The advantages of the combination tool or tools, and the kits which include combination tools, are small size and light weight. They are well suited to storage in the tool bag beneath the seat. Individual tools are easier to work with but make a far bulkier package.

Another outfitting strategy is to take your cycle down to the bike shop and select the individual tools required, or write to one of the mail-order houses, describing your machine, and have them make the selection for you. This approach can prove to be the most economical for you.

If your wheel is equipped with a derailleur, you will need a free-wheel removing tool if you plan to do your own free-wheel cleaning and relubrication. The type of tool you use will depend on the design of the free-wheel body.

88

If you plan to change rear sprockets on your multi-speed derailleur cycle, you will need a special tool for the job. The tool needed varies with the type of free-wheel body you may have. There are several types. In many instances you will find it simpler and less expensive to bring the bike to a shop that is properly equipped. There are so many variations that it is difficult even to come up with a general rule of thumb. There will, however, be many instances when you will desire or need to open and close the bike chain. To do this with a derailleur chain requires a chain rivet extractor. The style with the long handle requires no vise.

REPAIR TIPS

The business of right-hand thread and left-hand thread, coupled with clockwise rotation and counterclockwise rotation, can be a bit confusing. All it means is the direction the nut or bolt will travel when you are looking it in the eye and you turn it to your right, or clockwise. If the thread is right-handed—and almost all, but not all, are right-handed—the bolt will travel away from you. If it is a nut on a fixed bolt, the nut will travel away from you.

In Figure 22 we are looking directly down on a bolt head. As we turn it to the right, the bolt moves down. Figure 23 shows us a side view of the same bolt. It is still turning to the right and still moving down. When it gets the rest of the way, as indicated by the dotted lines, the bolt will be "tight." In Figure 24 we have a nut on a bolt. The thread is right-handed. When the nut is turned to the right, it goes down until it reaches the bottom and is "tight." Figure 25 is a fooler. We have a bolt with a right-hand thread coming up through a hole in a sheet of metal, as for example a mud guard. To tighten, the nut is turned to the right. The bolt must either be held

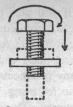

FIGURE 22. The metal plate is fixed. When the bolt is turned to the right, the bolt moves down.

FIGURE 23. Continued turning to the right brings the bolt all the way down until it strikes the plate and becomes "tight."

FIGURE 24. The bolt is fixed in the plate. The nut is turned to the right until it strikes the plate and becomes "tight."

FIGURE 25. The bolt is loose in the plate. When the nut is turned to the right, the bolt must be held immobile or turned to the left.

immobile or turned *to the left*—if you are looking down. All you have to remember is that the nut is traveling down, while the bolt is traveling up. If you bend down and look up, the bolt will need to be turned to the right, with the nut immobile or turning to the left.

When a nut and bolt have a left-hand thread (they must both be the same or they won't mesh), turning the nut to the right makes the nut come up—what we would call loosening. Left-hand threads are used on parts that normally turn to the left, as for example the left pedal and the left-hand side of the pedal crank shaft. When you pedal forward, whatever friction exists between moving shaft and left-hand nut tends to tighten the nut.

90

DON'T OVERTIGHTEN

A man of average strength with a foot-long wrench can easily snap a half-inch bolt of ordinary steel. If it doesn't snap, the threads may give way, which can be worse. You'll need to hacksaw the part free. Overtightening can also stretch the bolt, making it more liable to loosen than if it were properly tightened.

DON'T USE THE WRONG TOOL

For example, if your wrench is a bit too large for the nut, it will rip the edges from the nut when you exert pressure. If the nut or bolt is very tight and you use pliers, you will quickly convert the bolt to a length of rod; the edges will be removed. If the screw head is very large and the screwdriver point very small, you may ruin the driver or chew a little out of the screw slot.

FROZEN PARTS

When you encounter a nut or bolt that won't give at all, consider the possibility that you are turning it the wrong way before you give it all your strength and possibly snap the bolt in two. Try giving the threads a shot of "liquid wrench" or any of the other penetrating solvent lubricants that dissolve iron oxide. Wait a few moments, tap the parts a bit to make the liquid penetrate the cracks, and then try again. If you can't make it budge at all turning the correct way, try the other way. If it can be made to budge a bit, work it back and forth, adding solvent as you go.

DON'T CHARGE RIGHT IN

Repair is a science. Stop and consider how the mechanism is supposed to work, then try to determine why it is not working that way, before you change any settings. Just changing things will not accomplish very much, even though the device may start working again. You won't know what happened or how to prevent the malfunction from happening again. If the necessary repair appears to be difficult, don't do it until you are certain there is no other way. This should be your guiding principle. Most often the correct touch in the correct place will do the trick. So hope for the best; don't jump to the conclusion that all is gone and you have to take everything apart. Just keep trying the easy measures until you run out of them; then, and not before, is the right time to go the hard way. A good example that comes to mind is the derailleur: You can take the entire thing apart and put it perfectly together and still find it doesn't work correctly, when all it needed was an adjustment.

CHAPTER 7

Tires

There are four kinds or types of bicycle tires: pneumatics, balloons, clinchers, and tubulars.

PNEUMATIC TIRES

Pneumatics are one-piece tires. They are found on very inexpensive cycles made for children, delivery cycles, and the like. Pneumatic tires are tough, inexpensive, and comparatively heavy.

There are two means of repairing pneumatics (and a third, if you add bandaging the tire with friction tape, which we did as kids). Neither of them requires the tire to be removed from the rim. One is a brass arrangement consisting of a bolt with a hook and a large, flat, threaded-washer sort of nut. You clean around the puncture, salve the area with rubber cement, and insert the hook end of the contraption into the hole. The circular nut is tightened as far as it will go. A pair of cutting pliers is used to cut the bolt flush to the brass disk, then a file is used to smooth it further, and the job is done.

The second means will handle a slightly larger hole. It is accomplished with a sort of gun device. You load it with two, three, or more rubber bands and then coat the bands generously with rubber cement. Then the "trigger" is pulled. This stretches the rubber bands and makes them thin. The end of the gun is inserted in the hole. The trigger is released, and the gun is slipped out. The now relaxed rubber bands plug the hole. The excess rubber is trimmed off, air is admitted to the tire, and off you ride. If the hole in the pneumatic tire is too large for the rubber plug, there is no practical way of repairing it.

There will be times when the tire will not hold air, although there are no visible holes. This may be caused by a loose valve, a defective valve, leaky walls, or one or more very small holes. Since the valve is most easily checked, let's go to it first. (Remember the basic repair principle: Look for the easy way first.) Fill the tire with air. Place a drop of water on the top of the valve stem, after having first removed the dust cap. Does it blow bubbles? If so, the trouble (or one of your troubles) is at the valve. Borrow a Schrader valve-tightening tool from your local gas station man. Better yet, purchase two metal Schrader dust caps; the kind with the prongs on top. (See Figure 26.) These screw onto the Schrader valve stems, so you always have a valve wrench handy.

Turn the dust cap upside down, slip the forked end into the valve, and feel for the slot. Finding it, turn the valve to your right—screwing it down. If the valve is

Ordinary dust cap

Use brass dust cap as tool.

Valve screws to left

FIGURE 26. Schrader (American) tire valve with brass valve-wrench dust cap in reversed position above. Ordinary dust cap to one side. You can use a very slim screwdriver to remove the valve in an emergency.

loose, air leakage at that point may be stopped. If the valve is not loose, cross your fingers and unscrew the entire valve. It's a thin, spring-covered little thing. Remove it gently, blow hard on its side, and replace. Sometimes a bit of dust on the valve seat keeps it from closing completely. Incidentally, when replacing the valve, make it snug. Don't overtighten it.

Most likely, if the leak is in the valve, you will have to replace it. If you are running Schrader valves, it is a good idea to keep a small supply on hand. One valve size fits all bike tires using the Schrader, or so-called American, valve stems.

If the leak is not in the valve and the tire takes a day or more to go soft, you may have one or more small punctures, or the tire may be porous. To find these leaks, immerse the tire in water. If, like me, you aren't particularly neat, you can do this without removing the tire from the wheel or the wheel from the cycle. Let the tire sit awhile in the water and watch for growing bubbles. One way of speeding the process is to pump the tire up harder then usual. You may find that air is seeping through cracks in the tire walls because the rubber is very old or the tire has been run soft too long and too often. Junk it.

To remove a penumatic from its rim, remove the valve completely; this will let all the air out. Then roll the tire off starting on the side opposite the valve stem.

You should find a strip of cloth covering the top or nut ends of the spokes. If it has been ripped, or if there is no such protective tape, add one after making certain none of the spokes protrude past the inside of the rim. The tape can be positioned with rubber cement. When replacing the tire, reverse the procedure. Insert the valve first, then work the rest of the tire back onto the rim. Run a little air into it and bounce it up and down a few times to make certain the tire is not binding on the rim and that the stem points straight toward the hub.

You are supposed to shellac the rim before putting this type of tire on, but we always depended on the pressure of the air to hold it in place. Thirty or forty pounds is about right, and so long as it remains hard, the tire won't slip.

BALLOON TIRES

Technically, tires with a cross-sectional diameter of 2 1/4 inches (2.125) or more are considered balloons. Most cyclists, however, refer to any tire more than 1-1/2 inches in diameter as a balloon. Just why industry began manufacturing tires of this size is difficult to understand. Perhaps it was a part of the general scheme that led to producing cycles that look like motorcycles.

Anyway, balloon tires are tough, long wearing, and excellent on ice and snow and slippery surfaces. They have a large "footprint," lots of rubber on the ground.

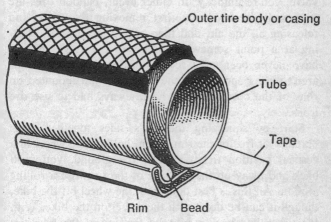

FIGURE 27. Basic parts of the clincher- and balloon-type tires.

And they are good for carrying heavy loads. They are tough to pedal, though, and you won't find an experienced cyclist using them.

Balloons are constructed like auto tires. There is a tough outer casing with wire "beads" along its edges. Air is contained in an inner tube. Recommended pressure varies from 22 to 30 psi.

Air leaks and punctures are treated as they are in an auto tire with an inner tube. If the air leak is slow, our first step, after inspecting the tire for nails and the like, is to check out the valve. This is done exactly as described for the pneumatic tire; the valve mechanism is the same. (Should the valve be a Presta—European type—read on; it will be discussed shortly.)

When the hole is in the tube, try to find the location of the leak if you can before going further. Listen for the sound of escaping air. Mark the spot. If you have but one puncture and you are lucky, you may not need to remove the entire tire and tube. If the hole is near the valve, you're unlucky. In either event, balloon tires are supposedly removed by first removing the valve and releasing all the air, and then rolling the tire off, starting at a point somewhere opposite the valve stem. I have never been able to do this. Perhaps my hands aren't strong enough, or the tires were not mounted on rims of the correct size. I have always had to use tire irons.

Start by squeezing the tire's sides together. This "breaks" it free of the rim. Then, holding the wheel in a vertical position firmly against the ground, you push back and away on the top side of the tire with a rolling motion. All this is best done with the wheel off the bike, though it can be done with the wheel on the bike. With the tire rolled back a bit, slip the end of the bike tire iron under the nearest edge of the tire and press down gently. Take great care not to catch the tube and not to push the iron much past the edge of the tire. This is easy to say but hard to do, because you cannot really see inside the tire casing. Pry the tire edge up and over the lip of the rim. Hold it there. Now slip the end of a second tire iron under the edge of the tire at a point some six to eight inches away. Pry the tire edge up and over the lip of the rim. Hold it. Push down on top of the tire with an elbow or chin. That will flatten the tire. Lay the tire on its side. Let one tire iron remain in place, and work the other one along until you have a section of the tire over the rim. At this juncture there should be sufficient space between the edge of the tire and the lip of the rim for you to slip your hand inside and pull out a portion of the limp tube. (See Figure 28.)

If you can see the hole, fine. If not, or if the hole is near the stem section of the tube, you will have to uncover more tube, and if you uncover half of the tube, you might as well take it all out. Remember, you do not have to remove the second bead or tire edge from the rim. Just let the carcass lie there.

Assuming you have elected (or have been forced) to remove the entire tube, replace the valve and blow it up fat, say to 1 1/2 times its in-place size. (Watch the tube and not the pressure when filling the tube alone with air.) Immerse the tube in water. A small pan will do, since you do not need to submerge the entire tube at once. When you find the leak, mark it with a large circle. You don't want pencil lead or crayon grease beneath your patch. Let all the air out of the tube by removing the valve again.

Dry the tube with a cloth and place the area to be patched on a flat surface—a table or what have you. If you have not removed the tube from the casing, slip a section of wood beneath the punctured area. Next roughen the patch area, which should extend at least a half-inch in all directions from the edge of the hole or rip. Use sandpaper, emery cloth, or a clean wire brush. Scrape away until the surface of the rubber is dull and rough. You don't need to dig in, but you do need to be certain to remove the fine layer of talc powder.

Apply a layer of rubber cement, Velox compound, or whatever cement comes with your tire patch kit to the area you have roughened. If the cement dries—loses its shine—in less than a minute, you haven't applied enough; add some more. If it takes more than two or three minutes, just wait until it is pretty dry—no shine. Now apply the patch. Your kit will have several round or oval-shaped patches. Choose the one suitable

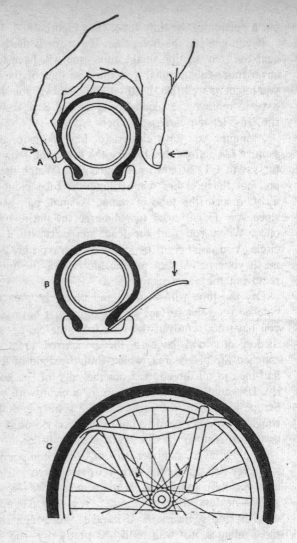

FIGURE 28. Steps in removing a balloon or clincher tire from a rim. (A) Squeeze the tire to break it free of the rim. (B) Slip a tire iron between the casing and the lip of the rim. Push down. (C) Us two tire irons to work one bead over the lip of the rim.

—larger by a half-inch than the puncture. If the cut is 1 inch long, you need a patch 1/2 to 3/4 inches wide by 2 inches long.

Auto-type tube patches may be used to repair the balloon tires, but the patches made for bike tubes are better because they are thinner. If one of the precut patches won't do, be certain to round off the corners of whatever shape you cut to fit.

Remove the glazed cloth from the face of the patch carefully. Try not to pull the patch out of shape. Then place the patch face down on the cemented area, taking care to press it evenly onto the cement. Now rap the patch with the back of a screwdriver or light hammer to force the patch tightly against the tube. Wait a few minutes, replace the valve, refill the tube with air, and give it another water test. The most frequent cause of patch failure is applying the patch before the cement has dried.

You will be surprised by the size of the hole you can seal if the rubber is in good condition and you prepare it as directed. If the rubber is porous with lots of tiny holes, forget it. If the leak is at the valve stem or very close to it, it cannot be repaired either.

Examine the inside and outside of the casing carefully before replacing the repaired tube. Look for nails, pieces of glass, holes, and breaks in the casing wall. If there is a small hole, say under a quarter-inch in diameter, cement a patch to the inside of the tube. Use a patch made for the purpose. It is shaped somewhat similar to a section of the tube. It is called a boot. When the break in the casing is larger, when it consists of break lines radiating from the hole, it is best to junk the tire—though I have seen balloons with boots that went all the way around the inside of the casing. Such tires are hard to pedal, and they shake as they roll.

Before the tire—tube in position—is replaced on its rim, the outer circumference of the rim should be inspected. If the rim tape is firmly in place, run your fingers over it to make certain that none of the spokes are projecting past the nipples or long nuts that join the spokes to the rim. Should you encounter a high spoke end—higher than the nipple—cut it back. Use a file or a small power-driven grindstone. The kind that fits onto an electric drill is fine. Just watch your eyes when the metal particles fly.

If there is no rim tape, install one. If you have no tape handy, a layer of rubber electrician's tape will do. Use a small, sharp knife to cut the hole for the valve stem after you have positioned the tape. If you do have rim tape, use rubber cement to mount it.

We now have an airtight tube, a casing free of holes, bits of glass, and other troublesome material, and a wheel with an outer rim free of spoke ends, said rim covered with protective tape. Next we apply some talc powder to the inside of the casing, especially to the edges of a boot we may have installed, and some talc to any and all patches we may have made to the tube. The talc—just plain old baby powder—prevents the rubber-cemented edges from sticking. It also lubricates the tube, making it easier for you to get it in place and for the tube to adjust itself after the tire has been assembled.

If you have removed the casing and tube completely from the wheel, this is how you will remount the tire. If you have only partially removed the tire from the wheel, pick up the instructions when they reach your condition.

Start by replacing the valve and running a little air into the tube, just enough to give it form. Slip the tube into the casing. To mount the tire, you need to get both casing beads inside the lips of the rim. Trying to work with both beads at once is the hard way. Work with one

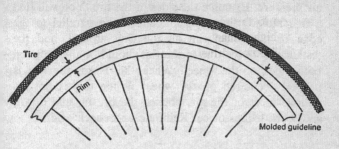

FIGURE 29. Make certain the tire is centered by seeing that the guide line runs parallel to the rim and that the distance from rim to guide line is the same on both sides.

at a time, and keep the other away and clear.

Begin at the valve stem. Push the stem through the hole. If it had a lock nut, replace it. The nut will hold the tube in place for you. If not, you will have to tug at the stem now and again as you work, to keep it from slipping inside. Next push that section of one bead that is immediately behind the stem down and inside the rim lip. Hold it there while you work around the rest of the casing, pushing and prying the bead behind the near lip of the rim. You may need to use a tire iron to get the last section in place. Be careful: You don't want to catch the tube between the tire iron and the wheel at this stage of the game.

One bead safely in place, juggle the wheel to settle the tube. Hold on to the valve stem. Put the wheel back on the floor or work bench, and attack the second bead, starting behind the valve again. This will be harder, and you will have to use the tire irons sooner and take even more care with the tube.

When the tire is back on the wheel, check the valve stem. If it is not pointing directly toward the hub, bounce the wheel up and down a few times while you tug at the stem and straighten it. Fill the tire to its rated air pressure. Examine the sides of the tire. You will find a fine molded line. The line should be parallel to the edge of the wheel rim all the way around, and the distance from the line to the rim should be the same on both sides of the wheel. When this is so, the tire is properly centered on the wheel. When this is not so, remove most of the air, bounce the tire up and down, and work it into place. Reinflate and check again.

CLINCHERS

Sometimes called wired-ons, clinchers are similar to balloons in that they too have tough outer casings and thin, rubber inner tubes. Clinchers differ from balloons in weight, size, and the fact that some clincher tubes are fitted with Presta valves, which cannot be aired with Schrader American fittings. (Although American air hoses and air pump connections will not fit Presta valves and neither will pumps terminating in Presta fittings work with American valves, it is a low-cost matter to purchase adapters which will enable one type of connector to work with another type of valve.)

Clinchers vary in width from 1 1/4 to 1 3/4 inches. They are far and away the most practical tires for touring and pleasure riding. The lightweight clinchers are only a few ounces heavier than the heavy tubulars, and the 27-by-1 1/4-inch clinchers can be pressured to 85 psi, which makes them almost as hard and as easy-riding as the tubulars.

Presta valves differ from American valves in that the Presta has no inner spring; air pressure alone keeps it closed. To fill a tube with a Presta valve, one removes the dust cap and unscrews the little cap that is exposed.

Not until this is done can air be admitted or released from the Presta valve. (See Figure 30.) Presta fittings—the end of the pump from which the air is expelled—are rubber-lined and are pressed into place over the valve stem and held there with one hand (as illustrated in Figure 31). After the tire has been pumped up, one knocks the fitting off. Don't wriggle it off since that strains the valve stem. After the pump is removed, the little knurled cap is tightened. This closes the valve, but don't rush; there is an inner valve which prevents the air from escaping. The little cap merely locks the valve closed. Should the inner valve fail (meaning should it let air out when the top cap is loose), push the little stem in and out when the tire is under pressure. This may remove dust from the valve and cure the trouble.

To release air from a tire with a Presta valve, unscrew the little cap as far as it will go, and hold the little rod down with a pointed tool. The Presta valve is never removed. If it leaks, think about replacing the tube.

Punctures in clincher tires are located and repaired in exactly the same way as punctures in balloon tires. However, do not use auto-type repair patches with clincher tubes; these patches are too thick. Also, be far more careful with the tire irons. Clincher inner tubes are thinner; tire-to-rim fit is closer. Because the tubes are so thin, don't neglect the protective tape around the rim. It is also important with clinchers to make certain the tire is centered on its wheel, so take a very careful look at the guide marks.

When replacing a clincher tire, don't switch tire-section diameters. You cannot fit a 26-inch tire to a 27-inch wheel, so that can't get you into trouble; but you can sometimes fit a 1 1/4-inch-wide tire on a rim designed for a 1 1/2-inch-wide tire, and that can lead to trouble. Or you can possibly damage a 1 1/2-inch

- Dust cap
- Press stem to release air.
- Loosen little cap.
- Lock nut

FIGURE 30. Presta (European) tire valve

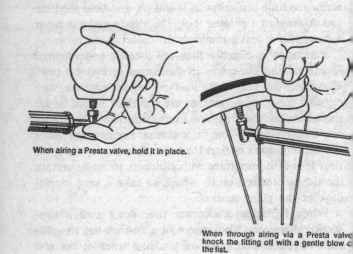

When airing a Presta valve, hold it in place.

When through airing via a Presta valve, knock the fitting off with a gentle blow of the fist.

FIGURE 31. Proper handling of Presta fittings.

tire by trying to force it on a 1 1/4-inch rim. At the least, an interchange can seriously curtail the life of your tire.

Another item of difference between the balloon and the clincher is that the baloon is mounted dry, whereas it is recommended that the clincher be fastened to its rim with shellac or wheel cement. This makes tire mounting messy, and I can't say that very many cyclists use shellac or cement to mount clinchers, but the cement will help hold the tire in position should you run it a bit soft. When the tire is very soft, nothing will hold it in position.

TUBULARS

Also known as sew-ups, sew-ons, and racing tires, tubulars have to be taken apart to be believed. The heaviest weigh less than a pound, and the lightest weigh some six or seven ounces including the inner tube. Tubulars are run at pressures of 70 to 120 psi, depending on the road or racing surface. "Tubs" give you the fastest, least comfortable ride, but even the lightest, made of silk, are much tougher than one can easily imagine. They are time-consuming to repair, but since they are lightweight, it is easy to carry spares rubber-strapped to the bottom of your cycle seat.

Tubular puncture repair procedure is as follows. The dust cap is removed and the little pin pressed down until all the air has been released. Beginning at the point on the circle opposite the valve stem, the tire is rolled back and off its rim. Remove the lock nut on the stem before trying to pull the stem out. The tire is inflated and immersed in water to locate the leak or leaks. The locations are carefully marked. The tire is dried, and the fun begins.

Inspect the inner circumference of the tire. You will

note that the cemented-on protective tape's end laps its beginning. If the puncture is close to this, carefully pull the inner tape back and off. If the puncture is not within a foot or so of the start of the tape, try a flank attack.

Take a flat, medium-sized screwdriver, and work its point under the inner tape as far as you can go, which won't be far. Then attack the same spot from the other side. Once you can get the screwdriver beneath the tape, you can pull it up by brute force. If you have to, use pliers to help you. Lifting the tape will reveal the stitching. Let the tape dangle. Use a razor, and carefully cut the stitching down the middle until you have opened a space long enough to permit you to insert your fingers and remove the punctured section of inner tubing. With the innards of the tire in hand, slip a small block of wood beneath the puncture area, and follow the same steps used to repair a puncture on a balloon tire. Just be certain to use the thin rubber patch material made for tubulars and to round the corners of any patches you have to cut from stock.

Should you fail to see the puncture in the tube, inflate the tire a bit and hold a wet finger over the area. If that doesn't tip you off, try a little soapy water. Just make certain the spot is dry and free of soap before you start patching. After the patch has been pressed home, sprinkle it with a little talc to make it slippery, replace the tube within the tire casing, and push the flap back into place.

Now to sew the patient up. You need silk thread and a large needle with a triangular cross section, since that shape passes most easily through the holes in the carcass. If you purchase a patch kit made by Dunlap, Velox, or others, you'll have everything you need. Before sewing, remove all the old thread ends, and line

108

the two halves up carefully; otherwise you'll get a lump and will have to do the job over again.

Use a simple overhand stitch and double thread. Follow the old holes and don't pull too tightly, or you will rip the tire casing. Don't use nylon thread; it will cut its way through the casing. Sew away until you come near the end of the open section. Push the rubber end of a pencil into the tire. This will hold the tube down and away from the needle. Sew as much as you can, remove the pencil, and finish the job.

This done, apply a generous coating of rubber cement to the inner surface of the tube where the tape used to be. Now apply rubber cement to the inside surface of the loose tape. Put a little air into the tire to give it shape. Wait until the rubber cement is almost dry, and work the tape back into place, starting at the attached ends. If there is a kink in the middle, cut the tape and lap the ends.

With the tubular tire repaired, your next steps are examining the rim and preparing it for the tire.

If you are going to mount tubulars sized 0, 1, or 6, you do not need to use a rim tape—a layer of cloth cemented to the rim. Should you be mounting tires of another size, you ought to use tape.

Should there be tape already on the rim, examine it carefully. If it is ripped, remove it, clean the base metal with a cement solvent, and dry. Examine the rim for projecting spokes, and file down if present. Apply a generous quantity of cement to the rim. Press a new tape in place, taking care to keep its sides a bit inside the edges of the rim. Let the newly cemented tape sit overnight if possible. When the tape is completely dry, give it a modest coating of cement. If you want to avoid fooling around with cement and all that, you can use Jantex, which is a tape that is permanently sticky on both sides.

You merely press it firmly onto a clean, dry rim. You do not use cement at all; the tire goes directly on.

If there is no tape, examine the rim for projecting spokes, and file if present. Remove any clumps of cement that may have built up in the rim with a cement solvent. Clean and dry. Apply a moderate amount of rim cement evenly to the rim of the wheel. Let the cement grow sticky or tacky.

At this juncture you have a limp tubular tire in hand and are facing a bare rim with sticky cement, a taped rim with sticky cement, or a rim with a layer of the aforementioned Jantex tape. Now to mount the tubular.

Make a pad from some newspapers, and place it on the ground. Rotate your wheel until the valve hole is on top, and set the rim vertically on the pad. Grasp the tire behind and above the valve. Give it a bit of a turn, and slip the valve in place. Spread the tire out a bit, and push down on both sides to stretch it. In this way you can work it down to almost the bottom of the wheel. Now comes the hard part. Standing up beside the tire, bend over it, and reach down to the remaining portion of the tire not on the rim. Turn this up a bit toward yourself, and push down a little on one side and a little on the other. The reason for the reverse turn is that you want it to roll over the rim and into place. This done, put a little air in the tire and roll the wheel. Inspect the valve stem. Make certain it is pointing to the hub. Now look at the sides of the tire, and see if the molded lines to either side are the same distance from the rim and that the lines run parallel to the rim all the way round. (See Figure 32.)

TIRE CARE

Avoid potholes in the road. Watch out for broken glass, nails, and dogs with sharp teeth. Don't jump the

FIGURE 32. One method of fitting tubular tire to a wheel. (*A*) Start at the valve. (*B*) Work both sides of tire down over rim, pushing a little to stretch it. (*C*) You can get the tire over the bottom of the wheel by turning the tread side up a bit and rolling the tire in place. (*D*) Or you can turn the wheel around and press down with your palms while pushing the tire up and on with your thumbs. (*E*) Make certain the tire is centered on rim—that the tread is evenly spaced from both sides of the rim. Check the position of the guide line.

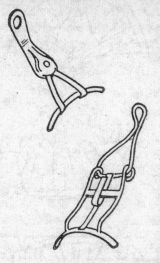

FIGURE 33. Thorn catchers.

curb, and don't run your wheel into a wall to stop it. This is fun at low speed, but beats heck out of the cycle. Above all, *keep your tire pressure up*. Soft tires are harder to pedal and wear faster because they flex too much. Soft tires will creep on the rim, bunching up and even coming off on a fast turn or short stop. See Table 4 for proper tire pressure. If you are a "fatty," add another five pounds of pressure.

If you are running on tubulars, it is advisable to reduce the pressure after finishing the day's run. This is something all professional racers do. The tire does not have to be emptied of air; just reduce from 120 or so to, say, 50 or 60 psi. Another trick racers use to extend the life of their tubulars is keeping them out of the sun. This may be of some slight value when the tire is of natural rubber but should make no measurable difference with synthetic rubber.

Some wheel men use "thorn catchers" to keep small objects from sticking in the tire tread. The thought is that many punctures are caused by bits of glass and thorns which do not puncture the tire immediately but work their way inside as the tire rotates. The thorn catchers rub lightly on the wheel and brush small objects off.

AIRING YOUR TIRES

The necessity of matching the fitting (end) of the air hose or hand pump to the valve on your tires has already been discussed. If you do not have the correct match, you just won't be able to get air into the tube.

Be careful at the local gas station. Don't let the nice attendant touch your tires. The danger here is that it is possible to burst a bike tire if one is not careful. The local compressed-air tank at the garage is usually filled to about 250 psi. If you draw on this air without an automatic air-pressure valve in between, the tire will be filled beyond its rated pressure before the attendant realizes the tire is full. If there is an automatic valve, it is safe for balloons and low-pressure clinchers, but I would not use it to fill a racer to eighty psi or more. The reason is again the small air capacity of these tires. It is possible for a puff of high-pressure air to get past the automatic valve and damage a tubular. So it is safer always to hand-pump high-pressure clinchers and tubulars, unless you are at a bike shop with proper bike equipment.

The usual cycle-mounted pump is difficult to use. You have no other choice in the field, but if you have space at home, get one of those old-fashioned straighten-up-and-bend-down pumps or one of the new

113

TABLE 4. *Tire Pressures*

TIRE SIZE (INCHES)	AIR PRESSURE (PSI)
12×1⅜	30 to 40
16×1⅜	30 to 40
18×1⅜	35 to 45
20×1⅜	45 to 50
24×2.125	35 to 45
26×1¼	45 to 55
26×1⅜	45 to 55
26×1¾	35 to 45
26×2.125	35 to 50
27×1¼	70 to 85
27×1 (tubulars)	75 to 120

TUBULAR PRESSURE SPECIFICS

Hard, smooth, indoor track	Front wheel, 80–110, rear 90–120
Uneven, outdoor track	Front wheel, 70–90, rear 80–100
Road racing	Front wheel, 65–90, rear, 75–100
Touring	Front wheel, 65–90, rear 75–100

step-on-it floor pumps. These are a lot easier to work.

Don't use your talented fingers to check tire pressure. Buy a pressure gauge, one designed for bike tires. A good one costs two to three dollars, but it will save you lots of tire grief. Keep it with your tool kit, and take the time to measure your air pressure. Doing so can tip you off to a slow leak before you get into trouble. Expect a five- to ten-pound differential between cool mornings and hot afternoon measurements. Don't bleed the tires if the pressure goes above their ratings by a few pounds, and don't keep fussing with a ittle air each morning, unless you have tubes of natural rubber—they leak air.

Pressures should be modified to suit road conditions. However, 120 psi is maximum for tubulars, 85 psi is about maximum for lightweight clinchers. Follow manufacturers' recommendations, when available.

The modern bike wheel evolved sometime during the latter half of the nineteenth century and reached its present form early in this century. Changes since then have been almost entirely in degree and result from new, lighter, and stronger metals, more careful and precise manufacturing methods, and improvements in tire material and construction.

All cycle wheels are alike in that their hubs hang from a web of wires. The spokes that are on the bottom at any given moment do not carry any load worth mentioning. All cycle wheels ride on ball bearings. Figure 34 shows the basic bearing system. There are some minor variations. The figure shows the hub acting as the race, which is the curved section that holds the bearings against the cone. In a machined hub you will find that the race is a little round cup that slips into

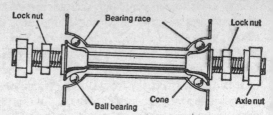

FIGURE 34. Cross-sectional view of the hub. This is the basic arrangement of parts used in both the front and rear wheels; however, the rear wheel may have additional parts.

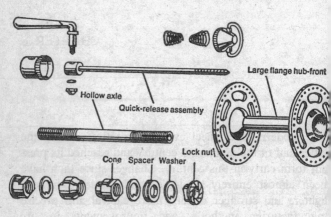

FIGURE 35. Zeus "Gran Sport" precision-machined hub front and quick-release skewer (lever) mechanism.

place. In a very low-priced hub you will find only one cone. The other end of the axle is carried by a "fixed" bearing arrangement. The bearings are in a little wheel-like component that slips over the axle and into a depression in the hub. You cannot err with this since it will not fit into the other side of the hub.

118

Quick-release hubs, as illustrated in Figure 35, have hollow axles to accommodate the quick-release rod that pulls or presses inward on the frame ends when the skewer or lever is turned. Regular axles are solid. The front hub shown will fit any cycle, the rear hubs are made for derailleurs.

It is obvious that the front wheel needs no more than the bearing arrangement shown and that derailleurs are actually outside of the rear-wheel hubs, so derailleurs don't interfere with the basic bearing system. But how about rear hubs with internal brakes—coaster brakes—and gear systems, and how about hubs that contain both coaster brakes and gears? The explanation is quite simple: The brake and gears are constructed around the axle bearings. The axle, cones, and races are on the inside and center of the hub; the balance of the mechanism surrounds them.

WHEEL TROUBLES

Cycles normally roll silently and smoothly. Should your cycle vibrate, shake, or make untoward noises when rolling down a perfectly smooth road, you have trouble, which may or may not be in the wheel.

Inspect the tires first. If a tire has been run soft, it may have bunched up at the valve stem. This portion of the tire will be larger in diameter, and the wheel will rise and fall as it rolls up and down this bump. If the tire has been run soft, it may have rolled. Sections of the tread which should normally be on top are now on the side. The tire is no longer symmetrical in respect to the road, and it causes the cycle to vibrate. Also the nonsymmetrical tire may be rubbing against a brake shoe, the frame, or mud guard.

If the tire is full of air and symmetrical, there is a

119

possibility that there is a boot (patch) on the inside of the tire's carcass, and the boot is either large or has come loose and bunched up. The level of sound and vibration caused by a boot may be very small and unnoticed in ordinary traffic, but it will draw attention when you first ride the tire down a silent country road.

Dry bearings will produce squeaks and rasping sounds. Very bad bearings will make the cycle difficult to pedal, and the wheel will have so much side play that it will drag against the brake shoes and frame.

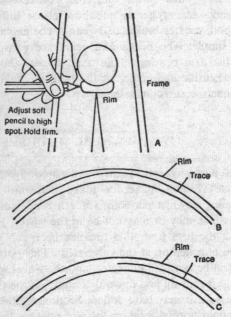

FIGURE 36. (A) Check rim for wobble and roundness. (B) Trace wanders up and down on rim. Wheel is out of round. (C) Trace misses areas. Wheel wobbles from side to side or is bent.

Vibration and shakes can also be caused by out-of-round and out-of-true wheels. These two conditions may be easily checked.

Turn your cycle on its back if there are no gadgets or controls that protrude beyond the top of the handlebars. This, for me at least, is the most convenient position for many bike adjustments and repairs. If you cannot flip your cycle, hang it up somehow, or lay it gently on its side. To check ovality (out-of-roundness), press the side of a crayon, colored lead pencil, or lipstick against the side of the front fork or rear stay, depending on the wheel you are testing. Press the tip of the marker gently against the rim of the wheel at a point near the lip of the rim. Spin the wheel slowly. If the wheel is perfectly round, the circle you draw will just match the circumference of the rim. If it is not, your line will wander up and down on the rim, as illustrated in Figure 36B.

Unless you have a new wheel with a machined hub, don't expect perfection. A slightly worn wheel with a pressed steel hub can show as much as a 1/16-inch variation and still be smooth-running.

To check for trueness (wobble), position your crayon in the same fashion. When you spin the wheel, let the wheel push the marker back if it wants to. If the wheel is perfectly true—flat—the fixed marker will make a line all around the rim. If the wheel wobbles, the marker will skip portions of the wheel, as illustrated in Figure 36C. If the wheel is badly out of true, you can see the wobble if you just look in a line with the wheel. Again, don't expect perfection. A little wobble isn't a bad thing, but any more than 1/8 inch between the high and low should be corrected. In other words, if you set your pencil just touching the high point of the wheel— that portion that comes closest to your hand—and then measure from the pencil tip to the section of the wheel

121

that is most distant, anything more than about 1/8 inch needs correction.

With the cycle flipped or raised for working, it is advisable to check front- and rear-wheel side play and rotational freedom. To check side play, simply push the rim of each wheel to one side. If you have top-flight machined hubs properly set up, there will be no side play. If you are running on loose cones, or are testing wheels with pressed-steel hubs, you can expect some side play. Maximum normal side play for properly adjusted pressed hubs should be no more than 1/16 inch.

To check rotational freedom, first look to make certain the brake shoes are free of the rims, then give each wheel a fast spin by hand. A free-running, properly adjusted, and lubricated front wheel should spin for one to two minutes and come to a stop with the valve stem at bottom. A free-running rear wheel will rotate about half this time. Incidentally, I mean one to two minutes by the clock. You can expect a little vibration induced by imbalance even when the wheel is perfectly round and true as you can discern by the simple pencil tests described.

WHEEL REMOVAL

To remove a front wheel, you need to loosen the two nuts to either side of the fork arms or pry the fork apart with a piece of wood if the fork arms terminate in holes rather than slots, and lift the wheel up and out (assuming the cycle is still on its back). If you have a caliper brake up front, it should be opened as wide as possible by means of the adjustments on the calipers. (See Chapter 9, on brakes, for details.) Hand-brake levers with quick-release features are lifted up and away from the handlebars, and the hold button is depressed. This holds the calipers in wide-open position for easy wheel removal. Should there be no quick-release feature on the brake lever, and should it be difficult to open the calipers sufficiently to permit the wheel to pass through, you might let some air out of the tire.

If you have a quick-release lever on the front axle, you do not, of course, have to fool with axle nuts. If you don't have the quick-release gizmo and want to avoid carrying a wrench, invest in four wing nuts—front and rear. You can loosen them with your fingers.

Rear-wheel removal depends on the power train and brake. Rear-wheel calipers are handled exactly as are front-wheel calipers. The presence of a coaster brake requires that the little bolt connecting the arm to the stay clip be removed. The presence of in-hub gears requires that you loosen the lock nut a bit and unscrew the rod found at the end of the gear-shift line near the hub. Should your cycle have both a coaster brake and in-hub gearing, you merely disconnect both lines or control cables as directed.

With one or both cables disconnected, loosen the axle nuts and gently move the rear wheel forward and up. When the axle is clear of the frame slots, lift the wheel up and gently remove the chain. The wheel is now free.

If you have a derailleur, crank the pedals and shift the chain onto the smallest rear cog. Open the caliper brakes as directed, loosen the axle nuts, and move the wheel forward and up. At this time you may have to press the tension roller down a bit to give you some slack on the chain. This done, you can gently lift the chain free of the axle and remove the wheel. If you need more slack, run the chain off the chain wheel.

One problem you may encounter in removing a wheel is a nut that has rusted tight—frozen—to the axle. Usually one nut can be loosened, because the other provides purchase for the second wrench. When one is firm, wrap some adhesive tape around the other end of the axle, and apply a Stillson wrench. The tape may save thread.

To center a wheel in the frame, pull up on the chain side until you have a minimum of slack. Tighten the nut on this side, even though the tire is to one side. Now use your fingers to center the tire, and tighten up on the second axle nut.

HUB DISASSEMBLY

With the front wheel free of the frame, examine the axle. If there are washers to the outside of the lock nuts, remove them. Turn the wheel on its side, axle straight up, after you have cleaned the hub of oil and road dust. Secure two wrenches, one to fit the lock nut, the other to fit the end of the cone. The wrench that goes on the cone must be slim enough to let the lock-nut wrench catch hold. (See Figure 37.) Hold the cone in place, and rotate the lock nut to the left. This will raise the lock nut. Take hold of the axle at the other end, and spin the lock nut and then the cone upward for about an inch. You will now see the bearings. They may be loose, or they may be in a little cage. In the latter case, memorize the side that is facing you. Lift the cage directly out. Use a small magnet to lift the loose bearings out. Put them in a little box after you have counted them. Now press the wheel down against the lower cone, and turn the wheel over. Lift the now-upper end of the axle. This gives you access to the bearings. Remove.

When the axle has been run loose for a long time and has spun in the frame, the threads on the axle will be worn behind the lock nut. In such cases it is probably not worth struggling to save the axle. Put the axle end in a vise, and cut if off behind the lock nut, or in front if

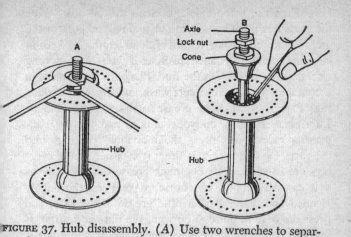

FIGURE 37. Hub disassembly. (A) Use two wrenches to separate the cone from its locknut. (B) After the cone has been raised, use a small magnet to lift out the ball bearings one by one.

you can get the hacksaw blade in without endangering the hub.

So much for taking the front hub apart. To do the same on a rear hub made for derailleur, the free wheel and the cog cluster must be removed in many hub types. This is discussed in Chapter 12, on derailleurs. To get at the axle bearings in a coaster-brake hub or a geared hub also requires a bit more effort. This is discussed in Chapters 9 and 13 on brakes and hub gears, respectively.

HUB REASSEMBLY

The inside of the hub and the bearing cones and all should be cleaned, lubricated, and then reassembled. Start cleaning by running a clean dry rag through the hub. Then use a toothpick to clean the oil hole. Wipe the parts down with a dry rag to remove the bulk of the grease and oil. Take another clean cloth, soaked in kerosine preferably and gasoline if you have nothng else, and run it through the hub. Place the loose parts in a container with the cleaner; wash and dry with a clean rag. Place a little light grease such as Gold Seal or Lubriplate Type A on your pinkie, and fill the ball-bearing races. Now press the individual bearings into the race. Do one race at a time; it is easier. If the bearings are in cages, force as much grease into the cage as you can after both, of course, have been thoroughly cleaned and dried. Add a little grease to the race, and press the cage in place. You want the flat end in first. If you are not certain, try the cone. It should slip into the race until its nut side is a bit more than flush with the hub. If it won't fit, the cage is in backward. Make the same check when the ball bearings are permanently inside the race, which is then slipped into the hub.

The bearings greased and in place, we carefully tighten up the cones with our fingers. When we have run them up all the way, we look at both axle ends. Are they about equal? Front hubs must be about equal. Rear hubs may require one end of the axle to project farther than the other. If the hub does not rest where we want it on the axle, now is the time to correct it.

Next we run both lock nuts up, again, finger-tight. A pair of wrenches is applied to one cone and its lock nut. The cone is held firmly while the nut is tightened against it. Going to the other cone, we use our fingers to take it up all the way, and then we back it off a fraction of a turn. At this point the lock nut is finger-tightened and the axle and cones turned. If it is still too tight, you will feel a roughness in your fingers as you rotate the axle. Loosen and back off as necessary.

CURING WOBBLE AND OVALITY

Rims that are out of true—wobble—and rims that are out of round can be corrected if there is no sharp bend. If the bend is abrupt enough to have deformed the lip or lips of the rim, if there is a secondary bump or deformation where the unwanted distortion starts, you are probably going to waste your time. Discard.

First remove the tire, and return the wheel to the cycle, leaving control cables and chains off if it's a rear wheel. You'll find it easier to work with an old extra front fork if you have it. The fork is mounted in a vise or pushed down through a hole in the workbench. Spread the fork with a block of wood if necessary to accommodate a rear wheel without rubbing. But since most of us don't have an extra fork, the cycle itself will do as the work and test support. A simple, easy-to-make test stand is described in Chapter 12, on derailleurs.

Examine Figure 38 before starting. Please note that front wheels and rear wheels not fitted with free wheels and gear clutches are centered within the frame of the cycle. Note that derailleur rear wheels are dished. The spokes on one side of the wheel are adjusted to a greater length than the spokes on the other side. The rim and its tire are offset in relation to the hub, but the rim and the tire are in the center of the frame. This is done to position the center cog of the five-cog gear cluster in line with the center of the chain wheel. That would be in line with a single chain wheel, with the juncture of two chain wheels, and with the center chain wheel of a fifteen-gear job.

Let us correct a bad case of ovality first. Using your reliable crayon, spin the wheel slowly, and find the high spot and the low spot. Loosen the spokes beneath the

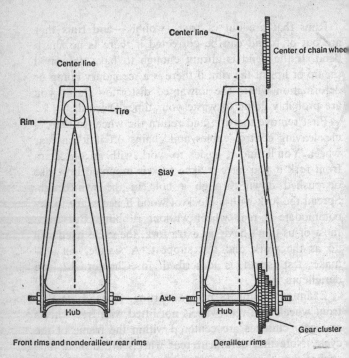

FIGURE 38. How rims are positioned by spoke adjustment over hubs. Note that the rim and tire are always in the center of the stays, and that stays carrying derailleur assemblies are more widely spaced than other stays.

high spot. Use the spoke wrench and not a pair of pliers. If the nipples are rusted, use some solvent. If that won't do, you will have to cut the spokes and repace them. You can cut them with a large pair of electrician's or side-cutting pliers.

Don't be too surprised at finding "frozen" spokes.

128

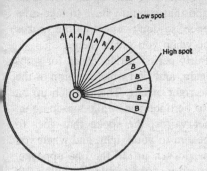

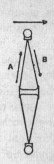

FIGURE 39. To cure ovality, loosen spokes A first, then tighten spokes B. Distortion is exaggerated, but helps to illustrate the need for tightening each spoke a different amount to make the rim round again.

FIGURE 40. Curing wobble. To move the rim in the direction indicated, loosen spoke A and tighten spoke B.

Unless you know the wheel struck a pothole or curb, you can bet that some lunkhead just tightened up on all the spokes. This would not have been too bad, but since some spokes could not be turned, tightening those that could distorted the rim. So when you go to work on a distorted rim, don't be surprised to find you need to replace several spokes.

After the spokes under the low or flat spot are loosened, find the high spot on the wheel again, and then slowly turn the wheel back and forth; using your crayon as a guide, find the center of the high spot. Tighten the spoke nearest this point first. Bear in mind that the rim will move radially about 1/8 inch for every seven turns of the spoke nipple. Remove the old crayon markings, and repeat your test for roundness.

You may find that you have to take up on more than one group of spokes and that you may have to take up a different amount on each, so don't expect all the spokes to "ping" like a chime when you pluck them.

With the rim in a fairly perfect circle, check for wobble. Use the crayon again, and find which portion of the wheel is too far to the right or left. Then tighten up on the spoke that needs to be tightened, while loosening up on the other. In other words, the spoke that goes to your right will pull the rim to your right, and when you tighten up on this one, loosen up on the one opposite. Generally one full turn on a spoke nipple will pull a 26-inch rim about 1/8 inch to one side, if the other spoke is loose. So if you have a rim that is 1/4-inch off, one turn should do it (think about it).

When you encounter a badly warped and distorted rim, loosen all the spokes, and remove the wheel from your testing jig. Use your knee and hands to take the side bends out, and use your body weight to push down the high spots after you have stood the rim on edge. Go easy. Do not attempt to correct the distortion with one push or pull. Take a lot of little bites at it. Put it back on the test stand, and check it out. If you get within 1/4 inch or so of true, make all the spokes finger-tight and check again. Then give each spoke a quarter-turn and check again. Repeat until each spoke will ping nicely when struck. Then quit. Don't overtighten, and don't be disturbed if some spokes have to remain relatively loose to keep the wheel true.

Dished wheels are treated exactly the same; you just work to a fixed amount of offset.

Don't try for perfection. Bringing the rim within 1/16 inch of perfection in roundness and wobble is pretty good. And don't tighten up on all spokes that don't sound tight. If a spoke is so loose that you can turn the nipple by hand or move the spoke up and down, take up on it, but check out its effect to make certain you aren't causing trouble. Of course you have to make certain none of the spokes have come up through the rim. If they have, file them down.

CHAPTER 9

Brakes

HAND BRAKES

Hand brakes are light, dependable, and effective. They are preferred by the experienced cyclist because they have no drag whatsoever. Hand brakes come in pairs, one for the front wheel and one for the rear. Each hand brake comprises a hand lever mounted on the handlebars and a length of control cable terminating at a caliper mounted on a pivot bolt. When the cyclist presses the lever by squeezing it against the handlebar, the caliper arms close and press the two brake shoes against the rim of the wheel.

Usually the brake levers are mounted beneath the handlebar grips when the cycle carries a flat or conventional handlebar. On turned-down, racing-type handlebars, the brake levers are mounted in front, above the gripped portion of the handlebars.

FIGURE 41. Hand-brake positioning on a racing cycle.

TESTING HAND-LEVER BRAKES

Operate each hand-brake lever. Note if there is any "hang-up" in its operation, if the action is sticky during pressure application or release. Then give each brake a very hard squeeze, though not as hard as you can—we don't want to break the mechanism. We just want to give it the pressure one might exert in an emergency stop. We want to make certain the cable and associate mechanism are up to the task.

INSPECTION

Carefully examine the ends of the cables where they come out of the tubes and the inside of the tube ends. This is where the cable emerges to join the hand lever at one end of the tube, and where the other end of the cable comes out to meet the caliper. It is at these two points that most of the wear occurs. If some strands have worn through and are free of the rest of the cable, replace the cable. If there is a deep groove in the end of the guide tube, replace it.

Inspect the brake shoes. There should be at least 1/8 inch of rubber showing above the supporting metal cup. Press your nail on the rubber shoe. It should have some resilience, like that of tire rubber. If it is rock hard, replace.

With the hand-brake levers in the released position—hands off—the distance separating the face of the rubber shoe from the rim of the wheel should be about 1/8 inch. If the distance is greater, make the necessary adjustment. If it is less and you haven't just

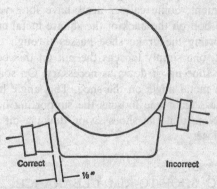

Correct   Incorrect
⅛"

FIGURE 42. Shoe-to-rim clearance. Left shoe is in the correct position. Right shoe is too high (it will ride on the tire) and too close.

tuned your top-flight bike for competition increase the distance.

Next try the front and rear brakes, and watch where the shoe strikes the rims. The shoes should be a fraction of an inch below the tire. They should meet the rim squarely. If the shoe grabs the tire, you will stop fine but your tire will be short-lived. If the shoe does not make flat contact with the rim, shoe wear will be uneven and braking difficult.

ADJUSTING SHOE HEIGHT

Let us call the distance between the shoe and the ground, shoe height. As stated, we want this height to be such that the rubber shoe rides on the rim of the wheel. When one cause or another changes the vertical relation between the shoe and the rim, correction is easily made.

All brake-shoe support designs have provisions for vertical adjustment. Some caliper arms have long vertical slots. The bolt on the back of the square metal cup or plate supporting the brake shoe passes through the slot. To adjust, one simply loosens the nut on this bolt and moves the shoe up or down as necessary. On some there is a little metal angle on the shoe. This angle has the slotted hole. Again one loosens the supporting bolt and corrects. Note that the shoes swing down a bit as the calipers close.

ADJUSTING SHOE-TO-RIM CLEARANCE

The normal wear of brakes, which results in greater clearance between brake shoe and rim, can be corrected in several ways. First, be advised that all hand-brake designs incorporate easy correction means. So look for the adjustment designed to correct for brake wear before you take anything apart.

Most often there will be no clearance adjustment on the shoe itself. Correction is made by varying the length

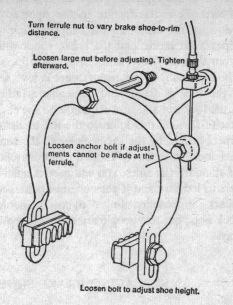

Turn ferrule nut to vary brake shoe-to-rim distance.

Loosen large nut before adjusting. Tighten afterward.

Loosen anchor bolt if adjustments cannot be made at the ferrule.

Loosen bolt to adjust shoe height.

FIGURE 43. The caliper arms can be opened or closed by adjusting either the ferrule or the cable. Try the ferrule first. Loosen the large nut, then turn the small nut to the right to open caliper.

of the cable or the length of the cable's protective tube. A word of explanation. Although the cable in its protective tube is flexible to some extent, the relationship between the inner cable and its tube is fixed. In other words, when you pull on the cable, you are pushing on the tube.

Actually you don't have to pay this bit of mechanical logic much mind. Follow the left brake cable to its termination at the front caliper. There you will find (in most designs) an arrangement of parts such as depicted in Figure 43. Loosen the biggest and outermost nut.

Now the ferrule, the metal end of the flexible cable, is free to turn. Turn the ferrule to the right so that it moves down. This will allow the caliper spring to open the caliper a bit more, and the brake shoes will move away from the rim. Reverse to close the calipers.

On the back caliper the arrangement is reversed. The end of the tube is fixed, and the cable is adjustable. Loosen the lock nut and turn the knob on the end of the cable itself. Turning this knob to the left tends to close the calipers and bring the shoes closer to the rim.

If the lock nuts have knurled circumferences instead of standard flat sides, you will need a small pair of gas pliers to loosen them if someone has tightened them with pliers. Supposedly, finger tightness should hold these lock nuts, but few people are willing to leave them that way.

REPLACING BRAKE SHOES

A bike brake shoe is a small rectangle of rubber either molded on and around a piece of metal fastened to a bolt or post, or slipped into a rectangular metal cup, also fastened to a bolt or post. Both types are replaceable. Just be certain to replace the bolt type with a bolt type and a post type with a post type.

To replace only the rubber rectangle you need a vise. Do not attempt to do it with the metal shoe holder in place on the cycle; you may very well bend the arms of the caliper, which in most instances will render it useless. Referring to Figure 44, note that the vise has been omitted for the sake of clarity. Slip the flat side of the point of a small screwdriver between the rubber end and the metal end of the rectangular metal cup. Push the old shoe out. Slip the new rubber in. When you replace slip-in shoes, be certain that the open end of the cup points toward the rear of the cycle. Thus friction

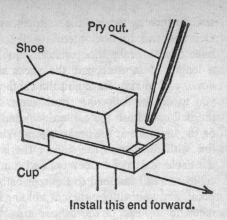

Labels on figure:
Pry out.
Shoe
Cup
Install this end forward.

FIGURE 44. Replacing brake shoes.

against the shoe, produced by braking, drives the shoe up against the closed end of the cup, and it is held in place.

CABLE REPLACEMENT

On some cycles such as the Raleigh, the front cable terminates in two lumps of metal—one a small barrel and the other a ball. There is no easy way, at home, of removing these cable terminations and later replacing them on a new length of cable, so don't waste your time fussing. Replace the entire cable and tube assembly. Usually the tube's inside is badly grooved by the time the cable has worn out.

If you have a brake system with permanently affixed end connectors, your first step is to remove as much tension from the cables as possible by adjusting the tube and cable ends at the calipers to open the calipers as wide as possible. Your next step is to ease the tension further by closing the calipers by external means. Get a friend to hold them together with his or her hands; use a brake-shoe squeezing tool, or simply wrap a length of tape around the shoes and wheels. This done, you will have a sag in the cable which will permit you to do the following: Push down and sideways on the ball end. Push the cable down and rotate the barrel on the two ends at the brake levers. When the cable is in line with the slot in the side of the hand levers, move the cable and barrel sideways and out. That leaves one cable end still fastened to the rear caliper. Look at that point, and you will see the nut holding the little block of metal to the end of the caliper arm. Loosen this bolt, and the cable and its tube can be removed.

If your cables do not have a permanent fitting on their ends but are clamped tightly under a bolt head, loosen the bolt and pull the cable out. When replacing, have the bike shop cut the cable a few inches longer than necessary. Slip the cut end of the new cable through the hole in the bolt and tighten as necessary. Do not cut the cable with an ordinary pair of pliers before you insert it. Once the end of the cable frays, you have a devil of a time fitting it into its hole. Expect to take up on a new cable after it has been in use for a while, because new cables tend to stretch a bit.

CABLE-TUBE REPLACEMENT

Remove the cable as discussed. Use care in removing the snaps holding the tube to the bike's frame so you don't scratch the paint. If the clips are held together by tiny screws, just loosen them. It is all too easy to lose these little beggars.

If you do not plan to move your brake lever, purchase a length of tubing exactly equal to that of the old.

Remember, for a fixed cable length, increasing the tube acts to bring the caliper arms together.

If your replacement cable tube is all plastic, there is no problem in cutting its end. If it is metal-lined, usually with a continuous spiral of metal wire, inspect the cut end carefully to see that no metal burrs project inward to snag and wear the cable. If the new tube is a little larger in outside diameter than the old, you can remove some material, if that is the type of tube it is, to permit it to slip into the ferrule sleeve. If the new tube is so small it can slip through the ferrule end, it's no good. Don't use it.

CURING STICKY BRAKES

In normal operation the friction encountered in operating a hand brake is negligible. So if the brake is sticky, doesn't respond smoothly when you press the lever, or stays closed after you release the lever, something is wrong. You have got to find the point of stick.

Start by releasing one end of the cable. If there is a permanent end, slip it out. If there is merely a raw cable, loosen the cable but do not let it come through the hole in the bolt. An inch of slack or so will do. Now try the lever. Does it stick there? This is fairly common. Some clod drops the cycle. The brake lever takes the brunt of the fall and bends its mount. Generally you can see the bent section if you look at the underside of the brake lever.

Sometimes the pivot or the pivot bearing (just a hole in the wall) is worn. Replace the bolt alone, and if that doesn't do it, replace the entire lever mechanism. Sometimes you can straighten the bent section out, and sometimes a drop of heavy oil will do it. But if you can actually see the wear, replace it.

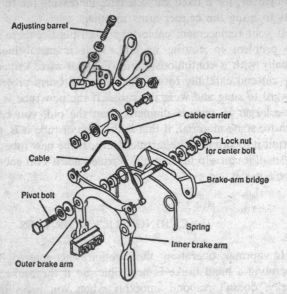

FIGURE 45. Weinmann "Vainqueur 999" center-pull rear brake, in approximate position of assembly.

Now go to the calipers. Squeeze them by hand. Do they spring right back? If not, use a screwdriver and carefully pry the spring away. Try the caliper legs again. Hard to move? Drop a little oil on it. Try to work it loose.

Try moving the large bolt in the center of the caliper. There shouldn't be any play. If you can move it, pull up on the nut at the other side of the frame (the nut that holds the pivot bolt). This may be very loose. Tighten. The legs should not be locked by tightening this nut. If they are, something is wrong; the parts of the calipers have somehow moved out of their correct position.

If oil or pivot-bolt adjustment doesn't cure the stickiness with the spring removed, take the caliper assembly apart, keeping close track of the sequence of parts. You need them all for proper reassembly. Clean with kerosine or gasoline, wipe dry, grease lightly, and reassemble. There should be a fine, thin brass washer between the caliper arms. If there isn't, I suggest you get one.

Note that the caliper assembly will have a little play on its pivot bolt. That will do no harm unless it is so great that the arms move sideways when the cable is pulled and does not bring the shoes into contact with the rim.

Another sticky point is the entrance of the cable into the housing. The cable will eventually wear a groove here. In such cases a little grease may act as a temporary aid. But with time the tube will need to be replaced. At this time it is best to replace both the cable and its tube.

Check tube mounting. Sometimes a fall by the cycle bends the tube ferrule, and the cable rubs harder on the edge of the tube than it should.

In some instances excessive friction between the cable and its tube and generally poor response in the braking action are caused by some well-intentioned ignoramus taping the brake tube tightly to the brake frame and handlebars, thus making the tube turn too abruptly. This too can cause a hang-up.

Sometimes friction between the cable and its tube can be cured with some oil. Turn the bike over or release the brake levers from the handlebars. Direct some oil down the cable tubes when they are pointing upward.

New cables should be lightly greased before insertion into a tube. Also apply a little grease to the cable where it comes out of both ends of the tube. This is the area that gets wet and picks up dust. A few drops of oil on the ferrule ends, the lock nuts, and other parts will keep them from rusting with time.

OFF-CENTER BRAKES

Sometimes you will notice that one brake shoe moves first to the rim, and that one brake shoe moves farther from the rim than the other when the brake is released. This is generally due to some stickiness in the pivot. Usually a few drops of oil will cure it. If it is very bad, you will have to disassemble the calipers as discussed.

UNEVEN BRAKE-SHOE WEAR

This may be due to a sticky caliper or a nontrue wheel. The wheel wobbles from side to side and rubs lightly on one brake shoe, wearing it down first.

PEDAL BRAKES

Pedal brakes are usually called coaster brakes, New Departure brakes, or Bendix brakes. When your bike has one, you can stop its forward motion by pedaling backward. About half a backward turn engages the brake and slows the rear wheel. The harder you press backward on the pedals, the more braking action you get. With pedal brakes in good condition, it is easy to put the bike into a rear-wheel skid, which is a simple test for brakes of this type.

Pedal brakes are not nearly as complicated as single-side-band receivers, color TV, or proportional electric typewriters, but they are complicated enough.

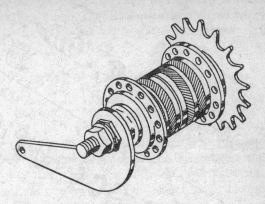

FIGURE 46. Assembled Bendix coaster brake.

Unless you have lots of patience and plenty of mechanical savvy, it is best not to fool with them. There are many, many different types on the market, each one coming apart a bit differently, and each adjusted somewhat differently. If you'd like to give it a go, what you need is a guide for your particular bike's brake system. Write to the manufacturer of your cycle—I'm not promising, but it is worth writing for. See the listing at the end of this book.

HOW THEY WORK

There are two general designs of in-hub brakes. One type, Bendix, uses two cones that come together and push a flexible brake band out and against the inside of a tube within the rear hub. The tube is locked to the bike frame via the brake arm. The other, New Departure et al., uses a pile of washers on the axle. When energizing this design the washers are squeezed together

145

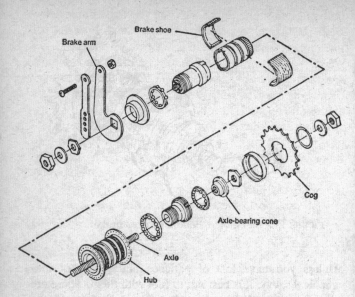

FIGURE 47. Bendix coaster brake in approximate position of assembly.

and press against one end of a tube within the hub. The tube cannot rotate because it is locked to the frame with the brake arm.

Now we must explain how the cyclist can brake and disengage when he chooses and how the wheel is freed to roll forward independently of the pedals when the cyclist rolls downhill and merely stops pedaling.

Forgetting the actual mechanism for a moment, let us imagine a large, heavy nut on a large machine screw. There is nothing holding the nut in place except its weight. The bolt and its thread are free to rotate. If we turn the bolt slowly in one direction, the nut will rotate with the bolt. If we rotate the bolt rapidly in one direction, say to the right, the nut will not turn as fast as the bolt and will move to the right on the bolt. Rapid left-hand rotation produces the opposite effect. Now let us put the bolt and its nut in a tube filled with grease. When we turn on the bolt, the grease drags on the nut. A rapid right-hand turn of the bolt moves the nut to our right. Left-hand turning produces a leftward movement of the nut on the bolt.

Let us drill a long hole through the length of the bolt, put an axle through the hole, and mount the axle on the frame of our cycle. We put a cog on the bolt and connect this to the cycle chain. Now we put the whole gizmo inside the hub on our rear wheel.

When we pedal forward, the nut moves to the right inside the hub. Here we set up corrugations on the nut end and the inside of the hub. So when the nut moves to the right, it locks to the hub, and pedaling forward turns the wheel forward.

Next we place a handful of washers on the bolt to the left of our nut. When we pedal backward, the nut moves to the left and presses the stacked washers to the left. This presses on the left end of our tube where we have mounted the end of the arm connected to our frame. Thus we get braking action by back-pedaling. This would be the New Departure design.

Following the Bendix design, we would have a nut with a cone-shaped left side. This would push against a brake band which expands against the inside of the hub. The left end of the brake band is tied to the frame with the brake arm. So braking is accomplished by back-pedaling.

To coast we merely let our feet rest on the pedals. This moves the nut from its engaged position a little to the left, and the wheel is free to roll.

All this is simple enough. Trouble comes with lack of definite information on wear characteristics. Put simply, without knowledge of proper spring tension, proper brake disk and belt thickness, cone wear, and the rest, it becomes a guessing game.

It is this writer's belief that the cyclist is best advised to pay the expert in the bike shop to take the rear wheel down once a year, if he is an active cyclist, and clean and regrease the coaster brake. It will leave lots more time for cycling. However, should the brake be operating in a defective manner, there is no harm in attempting a repair if it is confined to reassembly and bearing-cone adjustment.

Should the brake arm come loose from the bike frame, the brake will not work. Find the clip and bolt it back on again. Should the brake arm come off the brake assembly shoulder, slip it back on. If the wheel wobbles and has excessive side play, take it down far enough to find the bearing cones—they have a set—and readjust as described in Chapter 8, on wheels.

Don't condemn the brake out of hand. Some difficulties can be caused by external factors. An overly tight chain will make cracking and grinding noises; so will a new chain on an old cog and a chain with a broken link. An overly tight chain can also cause erratic braking in some types of brake design. A very loose chain can cause the brakes to grab. The braking mechanism is moving too fast because of the extra play.

LUBRICATION

The hub brake should be dismantled and greased about once a year if it is frequently used. Some manufacturers' literature says that once in two years is enough if the cycle doesn't see many miles.

Some of the hub brakes have oil cups, which makes it possible to keep them fairly well lubricated between grease jobs and perhaps can extend the greasing interval. I say "perhaps," because there is no published information on this subject and experienced bike mechanics I have spoken with have no "hard" data either.

Some brakes of this type do not have any means of lubrication. The manufacturers making this type of hub brake state that light oil, SAE 30, can be applied to the ends of the hub, where it will work its way inside where needed. Perhaps some will, but with this design you'd best take the brake down every year without fail.

CHAPTER 10

Pedals and Cranks

PEDALS

There are two kinds of pedals. One is called American and the other European. The only real difference between them, in addition to price, is that they come apart somewhat differently. Both types, as well as their variations, use the same cone and bearing arrangement, with a minor variation that is found in the wheels. The low- and medium-priced pedals—which in cycle language means heavier, less carefully made—are constructed according to the American design. The more expensive, lighter, and freer-running pedals are European-styled.

Should you begin to wonder why this book does not "tell it like it is"—two turns to the right on A, three turns and one zip to the left on part B—and instead insists that you actually pay attention, be advised that it is *never* like it is. There are millions of bikes scorching the roads in every direction, with parts made by thousands of companies, assembled every which way. No single set of directions would fit more than a road full of bikes. We can't give you directions, but we can teach you how to read maps and use a compass.

It isn't necessary to remove a pedal to get at the bearings for cleaning and greasing, but should you be a perfectionist, or should you want to replace the entire pedal, this is how it is done.

Get a pedal wrench of the correct size. A pedal wrench is simply a slim, open-end wrench that fits over the flat spot on the pedal axle at the end of the crank arm. A standard open-end wrench or a standard crescent wrench will not work. Don't waste time bruising your little fingers trying to do the job with a pair of pliers.

The pedal under your right foot, if you are seated on the bike and not fooling around, has a right-hand thread. Unscrew this one by turning to the left. The left pedal has a left-hand thread; unscrew it by turning to the right.

PEDAL DISASSEMBLY, EUROPEAN STYLE

Figure 48 illustrates the various parts of a European-type pedal. With the pedal in hand or on the bike, loosen and remove the dust cover at the end of the pedal opposite the end of the crank arm. This cover will have a "nut"-shaped end, or it will be knurled. In the first instance, you can use a wrench or pliers of the correct size; in the second, you will need pliers. Both left and right pedals have right-hand-threaded dust covers. In some far-out instances, you may find a dust cover that is simply pressed on. This type is pried off, but make certain you have turned it a few dozen times in

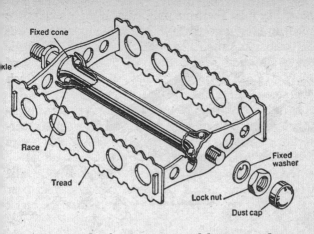

Fixed cone

Axle

Race

Tread

Fixed washer

Lock nut

Dust cap

FIGURE 48. Innards of a European pedal. Remove dust cap to get at the locknut. Center barrel, end races, and tread are one piece.

both directions before your pry.

Once the dust cover is removed, you will see the usual nut and washer; remove them. This will uncover the rear of the single, adjustable bearing cone. Back it off, and catch the bearings as they fall from both ends of the pedal. The pedal is apart. Remove it from the axle.

Clean the bearings and races and cones. Inspect the bearings and races for wear. Apply a thick layer of grease to the races, implant the bearings in the grease, and reassemble the pedal. Using your fingers only, tighten the cone as far as it will go and back off about a quarter-turn. Install the washer. Some washers used here are of the nonrotating type. They have either flat sections on the inner edge or projections on their inner edge. These "flats" and projections engage flats and slots on the axle, preventing the washers from turning

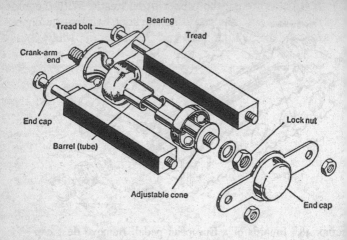

Tread bolt

Bearing

Tread

Crank-arm
end

End cap

Lock nut

Barrel (tube)

Adjustable cone

End cap

FIGURE 49. American pedal. End cap is removed to get at the locknut holding the adjustable cone.

when you turn the nut. Just spin the washer on the axle until the no-spin dingus fits the axle.

The nuts have to be tightened, and the first time you do so, you may find that the pedal will not rotate very easily or rotate at all, though it was fine when you tried the pedal before tightening the locknut. Don't worry. Just loosen the cone a fraction of a turn, and replace and tighten the locknut.

PEDAL DISASSEMBLY, AMERICAN STYLE

Take hold of the end of the pedal, the part opposite the crank arm. You will notice that this end section is all of a piece, as shown in Figure 49. To disassemble the pedal, this end piece must be taken off. Simply loosen and remove the two nuts holding the two bolts that pass through the rubber pedal treads. With the end piece off, you can get to the locknut holding the cone. Loosen the locknut, and back the cone off while holding the tube or center section of the pedal in place—firmly against the front of the pedal. The rear bearings will now fall out. Move the tube back, and the front bearings will fall out. Slip the tube off, and the pedal is disassembled.

As you can now see, the front bearing race and the rear bearing race are positioned by the tube. The treads, the part that makes contact with the feet, ride on the dust-cover arms. In the European design the tube and tread are one.

The American-design pedal is cleaned and reassembled exactly like the European type. Grease (Gold Seal or Lubriplate) is used to hold the bearings in place. The cone is finger-tightened and tried, and then the lock washer and nut are put in place.

You should expect a little side play in the pedals. If you have to choose between side play and a free-spinning pedal, take the side play. There is no harm in it; the grease will just drip out more rapidly.

CRANKS

There are three basic crank configurations: those with cotter pins, those without cotter pins (called cotterless, of course), and those made of a single piece of metal (arms and axle are one). The first two types have crank arms which are fastened to the crank axle, either by cotter pins (cottered type) or without cotter pins (cotterless type). The chain wheel bolts to the arm that fastens to the right end of the axle.

To remove a cottered arm, loosen the nut on the end of the cotter pin, or tapered pin if you will. Run the nut up until its top is flush with the top of the pin, then tap

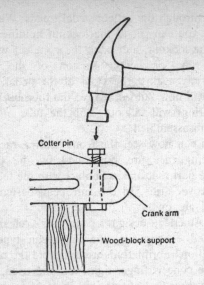

FIGURE 50. How the cotter pin may be removed. Bringing the nut to the top of the bolt prevents hammer taps from damaging the threads.

both very gently toward the axle. If the pin won't budge, try a little rust solvent. If that won't work, try a little heat. As a last resort, raise the end of the axle on a supporting block of wood and try tapping some more. *Do not rap the pin without backing it up.* If you damage the bearings, you will have to replace the entire assembly. When the arms are off, remove the chain.

A cotterless crank requires a cotterless crank-removal tool. (See Chapter 6, on repairs.) Remove the chain, then remove the dust cap. This may be pressed into place or screwed into place. Try unscrewing it first. With the dust cap removed, you will be able to get at the head of the bolt you see there. This will require a socket wrench of the correct size. If you have the cor-

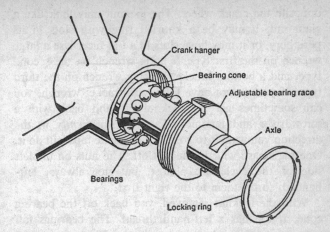

FIGURE 51. Left side of the crank axle, designed to accept a cottered crank arm.

rect combined tool, it will fit the dust cap and the arm bolt. Remove the bolt; just unscrew it. Next adjust your tool so that the large-threaded hicky is at the end of the bolt. Screw the threaded section into the crank arm. Make it snug. It doesn't have to be tight. Then turn the center bolt down and into the axle. When this bolt goes down, it pulls the crank arm up and away from the axle. Once you have seen the cotterless crank-removal tool in action, you will realize just how simple it all is. In effect, you are pulling the tightly fitted crank arm off the square-ended shaft. In some instances it will come right off with a little wriggling. Don't try to rap it off by hammering down in the center of the crank arm. You will damage the bearings.

With both crank arms loose—with or without cotter pins—the following steps are taken to remove the axle and its bearings for their biannual cleaning and greasing. Loosen the locknut. You will find this on the side opposite the crank wheel. The locknut may look like a giant nut, it may be a knurled ring with slots in its periphery, or it may have slots in a flat face. Use a large wrench on the first type, a hook wrench on the second type, and a bottom bracket bearing wrench on the third type. If you do not have a bottom bracket wrench, you can sometimes get the locknut off and back with a screwdriver and hammer. Tap the slot *gently* in the direction you want it to go. A lot of gentle taps will do it. One big smash will rip the slot off. The nuts on the left side of the cycle are almost, but not always, left-handed, so try them to the right first.

With the locknut removed, you back off the bearing cone. It too has a left-hand thread. The bearings fall out; you catch them and count them. Then remove the axle, tilt the cycle, and catch the bearings that were on the right-hand side of the axle. Some designs use caged bearings, which are a lot easier to handle, and some have needle bearings, which look like a row of pins set in a circle. These are held in a cage, too, so they are no problem.

If the crank hanger is full of lubricant, there is probably no need to remove the fixed cup or race at the other end of the hanger. It is the one whence the axle just came, so there is no possibility of mistake. If you have reason to believe the bearings ran dry, it is best to remove the "fixed" race and examine it. This race is right-handed. You turn it to the left with whatever tool suits it. Most often it will take a large wrench.

You will now have all the parts of the cottered and cotterless crank assembly apart. The chain wheel will be fastened to the right-hand crank arm. There is no reason to trouble it. Wash the bearings and races. Examine them for wear, and replace if necessary. Before we discuss reassembly, we have to go back to the one-piece crank and axle.

If you have the one-piece crank, there will be no cot-

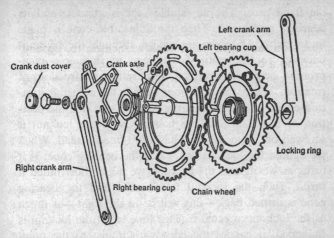

Left crank arm

Left bearing cup

Crank dust cover

Crank axle

Right crank arm

Right bearing cup

Chain wheel

Locking ring

FIGURE 52. Exploded view of a Stronglight crank set. We are looking at it from the right-hand side, and the "fixed" race is the one closest to us. No bearings are shown.

ter pins and no dust covers where the crank arm joins the axle. The crank arms and the axle are one piece of metal. So when you remove the left-hand pedal, you loosen and remove the locknut and the bearing cone, which is on the bike's left side. Then slip the arm and axle out the right side of the crank hanger. The crank wheel is part of the axle and arm.

CRANK ASSEMBLY

With everything clean and shipshape, we return the fixed race to the hanger, pulling it up very tight. Now we can either put the grease on the inside of the fixed cup and stick the bearings in there, or we can add a little grease to the axle and make the bearings hold on there. In either event the axle is slipped back through the fixed race. The adjustable race is greased and its bearings positioned. Then the adjustable cone is made finger-tight. At this point we go through the try-and-back-off routine until we succeed in finding a compromise between a perfect, no-play fit and freedom of rotation. When this has been found, we note the location of the adjustable bearing cone by marking the position of a slot against the hanger. Next the locknut is screwed on. Remember, it has a left-hand thread. When we tighten the locknut, we watch the bearing cone. If it turns as we tighten the locknut, we notice how much it turns. Then the locknut is loosened and the bearing cone is turned back—this will be to the right—as much as the locknut affected it. This time when the locknut is tightened, it carries the cone with it just to the point where we want it.

If you don't do this, you may tighten and loosen the cone and locknut a dozen times before you get the adjustment you wish.

CHAPTER 11

Chains and
Chain Wheels

The chain is that black, snakelike thing that connects the chain wheel or crank wheel with the back wheel. When the chain is in place, you go forward when you push on the pedals. When the chain is off, you don't go anywhere, except by walking.

Chains vary in pitch, width, and length. Chain pitch, the center of one link in the chain to the next, cannot be altered; neither can width. But a chain's length can be increased or reduced by adding or removing links.

Supposedly, all derailleurs are fitted with 1/2 x 3/32 chains. This means a chain with a pitch of 1/2 inch and a width of 3/32 inch. The "inch" sign is usually left out of chain descriptions. Coaster-brake, gear-in-hub, and sprint bikes use 1 x 3/16 and 1/2 x 1/8 chains. There are probably other sizes of chains, but these are the ones usually encountered.

You cannot interchange chains of varying pitch; they

simply won't fit on the chain wheel and rear cogs. But in a pinch you can make do with a slightly wider-than-original chain on a coaster-brake or gear-in-hub bike. On a derailleur, the overwidth chain will probably rub on adjoining cogs.

CHAIN REMOVAL

Many schemes are used to join chain ends to make the closed-loop drive chain used on a cycle: snap-on side plate, spring-connecting, offset, and force-fit rivet. These are illustrated in Figure 53.

The snap-on side plate is more difficult to find than to open. This plate looks like all the other links, except that it is a little larger. It is pried off with the blade of a

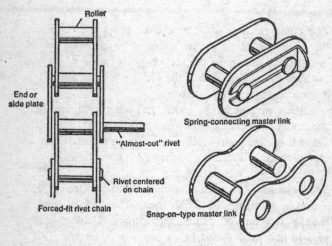

FIGURE 53. Three methods used to connect the ends of the drive chain.

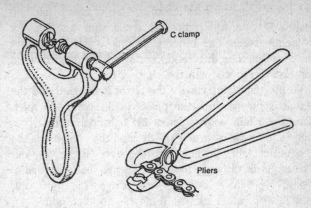

FIGURE 54. Cycle-chain rivet extractors. When ordering, designate chain size.

screwdriver and pressed back in place with one's fingers.

The spring-connecting arrangement is easier to locate, though it is the same color as the rest of the chain. Some of these spring gadgets are pushed back along the length of the chain, opposite the direction of the slit in the spring. Others are opened when one leg of the spring is pried up and over the rivet.

Generally spring and chain-end connections are found only on nonderailleur chains. Occasionally you will find a spring-connector end link on a derailleur chain. This is fine, if the spring does not rub the guide; if it does, you will have to remove that link. One link more or less is nothing in the life of a chain.

The offset and force-fit rivet connectors are used only on derailleur chains and are easily located. Actually this type of linkage isn't a connector at all; you simply "almost" remove any rivet in the chain. A special tool is used for almost removing and replacing the rivets. The tool comes in three general forms—pliers and two C clamps with handles. One C clamp has two positions—one for removing rivets and another for replacing rivets. The other C clamp rivet tool has but one position. The difference is that a little more caution must be employed with the simpler type.

To use the clamp device the chain is inserted and the handle is turned until the pin is in line with the rivet. Then the chain is wriggled a bit to make certain it is snug. The screw is turned slowly, and the pin pushes the rivet almost out. Do not push the rivet all the way out because it is difficult to get it started back in again. Should you lose control and drive the pin out, remove—or rather almost remove—another pin.

When the rivet is free of the roller, which is the tubular portion of the chain link, you can pull the chain apart. If it sticks, wriggle the chain a bit, but not so much that you bend the side plate. If you bend the side plate, discard the link. Should this happen often, you can purchase individual replacement links.

To reassemble the derailleur chain, reposition the side plates of the chain ends, and after making certain the rivet is at right angles to the chain, carefully and slowly tighten up on the chain tool's handle. Keep turning until the rivet is not only in place but extends out the farther side of the chain. Back off with the tool, and make certain that the rivet is centered in the chain—an equal rivet edge showing on either side.

The rivet pliers are handled the same way, but it takes a bit more skill to work the pliers and a lot more strength in the hands.

You can expect to go through the drill of almost removing and replacing a rivet or loosening a snap plate or spring on a chain every time you remove the chain for cleaning and lubrication and every time you replace the chain, every two to three years or every three to four thousand miles.

CHAIN WEAR

Wear can be judged by the feel of the chain and its growth. As chains wear, the play or clearance between each rivet and side plate increases. You can sometimes feel this "stretch" by pushing and pulling on a section of chain. You will also find that a worn chain is easily bent sideways, where a new chain is not. When the total play per length of chain is about a half-inch, the chain should be replaced. Measure chain growth by stretching the length of chain out on a smooth board and pressing the links together without deforming the chain. The length of the chain is measured. The chain is now pulled out and its length measured again. If the difference is more than a half-inch, junk. You can measure the chain on the cycle if you have an accurate means of measuring. Count off 24 links on a half-inch pitch chain. Measure carefully from the center of the end rivet to the center of the rivet on the other end. If you get more than 12 1/16 inches, the chain should be replaced. A half-inch of wear on a 5-foot length of a half-inch pitch chain is about 0.01 inch per link.

Still another method of detecting excess chain wear consists in wrapping the old chain around a new chain wheel. If badly worn, the old chain will be too large, and will not fit properly.

Chain lubrication is discussed in Chapter 5, on care of bicycles.

CHAIN LENGTH

On a nonderailleur bike there is no dither about chain length. The chain should be just long enough to permit a bit of slack when the rear-wheel axle and its washers are fully inside the slot in the frame. Chain slack is correct when you can easily lift the lower section of the chain about a quarter-inch.

Derailleur chain length is a mite harder to judge. The rear axle and its washers must be fully inside the axle slot on the frame. But the length of chain will vary with the gears you have selected for front and rear. You need sufficient chain to accommodate the largest of the front gears if you have more than one, and the largest of the rear gears, plus a little slack. When the chain is on these two large cogs, the two little wheels on the rear derailleur arm mechanism will be almost all the way forward. That "almost" is very important. If the derailleur arm, or jockey, is all the way forward, there will be no spring action to take up vibration. The extra half-inch slack is necessary to permit the chain to crawl up on the large cog wheels and down again without binding. You can check on the tension mechanism by simply trying to swing it a bit forward. If there is no spring left, the chain is short.

There will be considerably more slack in the chain when you put the chain on the smallest front gear and the smallest rear gear. The jockey will be all the way back (taking up the slack), and the chain will have about one inch of freedom. That is, you will be able to lift the lower section about one inch without pulling on the chain. (See Figures 55 and 56.)

Incidentally, the easy way to see all this is to lift the rear wheel of your bike off the ground. Hoist it up with a rope or make a simple stand of wood, such as the one pictured in Figure 57, that will catch the rear axle. You will need a long derailleur "protection" nut on the changer side.

The ratio spread between top and low gear is limited by the amount of slack the derailleur mechanism can take up. The number of gear steps is unimportant. Cut your chain to fit the largest front gear and the largest rear gear, plus the necessary loop and slack. Then

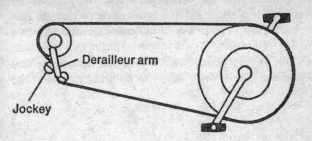

FIGURE 55. When the derailleur chain is on the largest front and rear cogs, the jockey is almost all the way forward and there is a little slack in the chain.

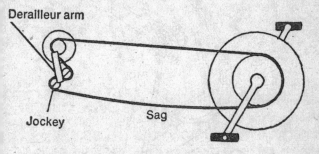

FIGURE 56. When the derailleur chain is on the smallest front and rear cogs, the jockey is almost all the way back and there is about twice as much slack. If there is so much slack that the chain tends to jump off the cogs, the difference in total size between the two largest gears and the two smallest gears is too great for the slack correction effected by the jockey wheels. This cannot be changed. Either decrease the size of the largest gear or increase the size of the smallest gear to correct.

switch down to the smallest front gear and the smallest rear gear. If you have too much slack, you must install larger small gears or smaller large gears so that the difference is less. The newer derailleurs can accommodate greater differences.

There is little chance that a bike sold as a complete, assembled unit will have this problem with its

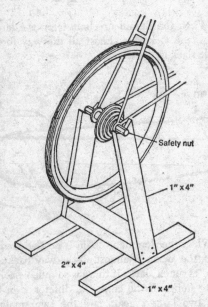

FIGURE 57. Simple rear-wheel test stand. You need the long protection "safety" nut on the chain side of the axle to reach the wooden upright. The safety nut prevents the derailleur mchanism from striking the ground, should the cycle fall to that side.

derailleur. The relation between gear-ratio spread and chain length is discussed here so that you won't seek nonexistent trouble in the chain or derailleur when faced with too much or too little chain.

CHAIN WHEELS

The chain wheel on the one-piece crank comes with the crank, and you must change it all if you want to replace it. The other assemblies have bolted-on chain wheel that can be removed and replaced easily.

When replacing a chain wheel, you must make certain its mounting holes match the holes in the crank and that the pitch (distance from point to point on a gear wheel) of its teeth matches the pitch of the teeth on the rear cogs.

You may want to change crank wheels to alter your gear ratios, or you may need to replace the wheel because it has worn out.

When the chain, the crank wheel, and the rear cogs wear at the same rate, the chain grows longer, but usually you do not have trouble until the chain is so long the slack cannot be accommodated. However, it is rare for all the parts to wear at an equal rate, so you will need to know what's to be replaced: chain or chain wheel. A simple test uses a length of new chain with a pitch equal to that of the drive wheel. Simply place the new chain on the old wheel and pull it tight. If the new chain appears to be "tight" on the old wheel, the old wheel is badly worn and should be replaced. A worn chain on a new wheel sort of bunches up because it is too long. To get the "feel" of a proper chain-to-wheel fit, try a new chain on a new wheel.

The teeth on a derailleur crank are only 3/32 inch thick at the tip. The body of the crank is not much thicker. When you up-gear, the chain is pushed onto the larger front chain wheel, and there is a moment when all the load is carried by one tooth. Should you slam the front gear changer, should you stand up and pump down on the pedal at the same time, you will bend the crank wheel. Should you drop your cycle or be hit by a runaway kiddie car, the crank will be bent. It doesn't take much to dent and bend a modern, lightweight front chain wheel. Once bent or dented, the chain rides incorrectly, placing abnormal and concentrated forces on the wheel. In addition, pedaling may be noisy and difficult. The chain may jump off unexpectedly.

You can readily examine the wheel for dents and bumps by deliberately running the chain off and sighting along the length of the wheel from behind. If you wish to be more exact, hold a soft, colored lead pencil to the side of the frame, its tip just touching one tooth of the chain wheel. Then turn the chain wheel slowly, and see whether the pencil tip touches each succeeding tooth as it comes round. To correct a dented chain wheel, remove and flatten by hammering it against a flat surface, or replace. Do not attempt to straighten it in position.

Coaster-brake and gear-in-hub bikes rarely have crank wheel trouble. The chain is not constantly shifted on and off its rim, and the wheel itself is thicker. But if one is bent, the same treatment is called for.

CHAPTER 12

Derailleurs

When you turn the pedals around with your feet, the chain turns the back wheel. If you have a large gear up front and a small gear in the rear, the rear wheel is going to turn faster than the crank. How much faster it goes—the ratio between crank turns and rear-wheel turns—is related to the ratio of the size of the chain wheel, which is turned by the pedal crank, to the rear gear wheels, which are turned by the chain. If you have just one gear wheel up front and just one gear wheel in the rear, you have a fixed ratio. To have a choice of ratios or speeds, you have to have more than one gear in the rear, or more than one gear up front.

In a five-speed derailleur bike you have one chain wheel up front and five little gear wheels or cog wheels in the rear. To change ratios and speed, you move the chain from one to another of the five gear wheels in the rear. You can do this by stopping the cycle, getting off,

171

and manually moving the chain from one wheel to another. You can also do this by reaching behind you as you pedal merrily along and, using a stick, force the chain to move from one cog to another. Or you can install a derailleur mechanism to do this for you. Actually, when one says derailleur one means the entire setup; rear cogs, free wheel, and changer mechanism, which is an improved stick affair.

Let us clarify the free wheel. It consists of two parts: an inner part that screws onto the rear hub and an outer part that rides on the inner part by means of ball bearings. The inner part is connected to the outer by pawls, which are little metal arms. When the outer part turns to the left (that is, backward when you pedal backward), the little pawls make a clicking noise. When the outer part turns to the right (forward when you pedal forward), the little pawls catch hold of the grooves in the outer part, and the inner and outer sections of the free wheel become one; as it is attached to the rear-wheel hub, the wheel turns with the free wheel. This arrangement of parts permits you to coast; that is, you can hold your feet still, and the back wheel is free to keep on turning. That's where the name free wheel comes from. The rear cogs are screwed onto the free-wheel body. When the chain pulls on the cogs, the rear wheel perforce must turn.

The rear derailleur mechanism does two things. It moves the chain from side to side, and it takes up the slack. Naturally, when you move the chain from the large rear cog to the small, there is more slack in the chain.

The best way to a quick understanding of what goes on is to lift the rear wheel of your cycle from the ground by means of a rope or the improvised test stand described in Chapter 11 ("Chains and Chainwheels"), and watch the derailleur mechanism at work. Turn the crank forward, turning the chain wheel and the rear wheel. Then hold the crank motionless; the rear wheel now runs free. Listen and you will hear the rapid click of the pawls as they slide over the teeth cut into the inner side of the free-wheel body. Turn the pedals again, and shift from one gear to another by operating the gear-shift lever. Begin at the high gear—the smallest—and go on to the largest gear. Go back to the small gear.

Notice that the jockey wheels—the pair of wheels on the derailleur arm—do two things. They move closer and farther from the rear wheel in response to your control lever movements, and they move forward and back as the chain slips down from the larger gear wheel to the smaller and crawls back up on the larger gear. Notice further that there are no "positions" as such on the control lever. You push the lever a little; the derailleur arm moves a little and the chain jumps from one cog to another, or two cogs to another or half a cog and slips back.

Loosen the little arm at the side of the control lever. The control lever jumps back and lies limp. The control lever is held in place by friction alone, controlled by the little knob. When the control lever is all the way down, the chain is on the largest rear cog. Let the lever fly, and the chain moves to the smallest cog because the derailleur arm folds back on its pantograph and moves away from the wheel. Do this several times until you realize how simple it all is.

In the released position, with no tension on the cable that activates it, the pantograph arm moves all the way into or against its support and is at the maximum distance from the rear wheel of the cycle. When you operate the control lever, you pull on the control cable, and the pantograph is extended and comes close to the rear wheel. There are only two adjustments on the derailleur pantograph arm. These are simply stops and are illustrated in Figure 58. One stops the pantograph

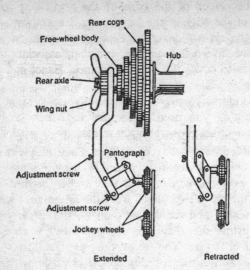

FIGURE 58. Simplified Huret derailleur (minus chain), looking rearward from the pedals. Left: Control cable is pulled. The pantograph extends until stopped by the lower adjustment screw. Note the jockey wheels in line with the large cog. Right: Control cable is released. The spring in the derailleur mechanism folds the pantograph, moving it just far enough to bring the jockey wheels in line with the smallest cog.

from going too close to the rear wheel, and the other stops it from going too far from the rear wheel. The close stop is set to permit the chain to reach the center of the largest cog, but no farther. Should it go farther, the chain would move past the large cog and slip onto the hub. The second stop prevents the chain from going past the smallest cog and slipping into the space between the small cog and the frame.

So we have a cable attached to an arm that pulls on a second arm that guides the chain from side to side a prescribed distance. This distance is the exact distance

174

from the center of the edge of the small cog to the center of the edge of the largest cog. Except for a few three- and six-cog derailleur designs, all derailleurs are five-speed, five-rear-gear jobs, and their associate arms are made to cover the proper distance. Exact swing is secured by adjusting the two stops.

Although there may be dozens of stop designs and positions, all you need do is turn the screw and see where the chain goes when you release the control cable and when you pull it all the way. Just remember that you are limiting its side travel in one direction with one screw. There is no control over where the cable lands between these two extremes. Cable landing is controlled by the friction-held lever up front. After a while the cyclist knows where this goes, just like a trombone player knows where his arm goes for A-flat.

The action of the tension and idler wheels, together often called the jockey wheels, has been discussed in Chapter 11. If you recall, the jockey is on a spring and it folds the chain up when its spring tension is greater than the weight of the slack. This take-up action is independent of the motion of the chain-mover arm in response to tension on the control cable.

So far we have treated five-speed cycles. To produce ten speeds or fifteen speeds, we simply add one or two chain wheels. Changing the chain from a wheel of one size up front to another-sized wheel multiplies by two the number of speed choices we have. Putting three chain wheels of different sizes up front multiplies our choices by three. The chain is moved from one chain wheel to another by the same arrangement of lever, cable, and moving guide arm as is used in the rear. The guide arm is moved from side to side and is again limited in its travel by two adjustable stops. A different guide-arm control mechanism is required, generally, when there are three chain wheels installed in place of two.

It is much more difficult to keep a fifteen-speed mechanism in admustment than it is to keep a two-chain-wheel, ten-speed mechanism in working order. The reason is that the chain must be moved farther from side to side and the angle, looking back at the rear gear cluster, is increased.

Now let us look at what happens up front when you have two or more chain wheels and you want your little gadget to move the chain from one to another. Hang the bike back up and pedal the pedals. Swing the front changer, lever down, pulling on its cable. Watch the front changer mechanism. It simply duplicates the action of the back mechanism on a smaller scale; it just doesn't move as far from side to side. Should you release the friction knob on the front changer control arm, the spring on the changer mechanism will move the guide mechanism closer to the seat tube. Again there are two control screws. One limits outward travel, the other limits inward—to the frame—travel.

ADJUSTMENTS

Assuming that the derailleur equipment has been properly mounted and that the chain is in good condition and of correct length, there are only four adjustments, as such, though there are several more you may want or need to make. The four adjustments are the ones we have just discussed—two on the front derailleur and two on the rear derailleur mechanism. All are best made with the cycle's rear wheel off the ground so that you can pedal and watch what happens. In the rear, you want the arm to move the chain from the largest sprocket to the smallest, but no farther in either direction, and you want to adjust the stops up front to do the same.

There are other adjustments. Most often you will be

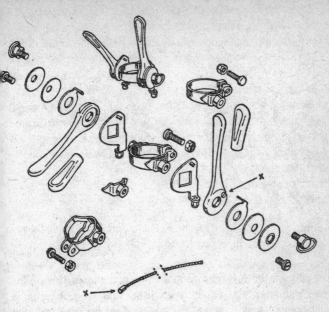

FIGURE 59. Huret dual-control levers. Parts are shown in approximate position of assembly. "X" indicates the ball end of the control cable which fits into the round hole on the control arm.

fussing with the friction controls on the shift levers. If there is too little friction, the lever moves of its own accord and you find you have changed gears. If there is too much tension, you will find it difficult to move the lever. Just turn the little knob at the base of these levers.

You may find that you cannot move the changers as far as you wish although you move the lever its full swing. This means that the cables have stretched or their housing has worn a bit. The easy way to take up slack in the derailleur control cable is to loosen the clamp that holds the control levers to the bike frame

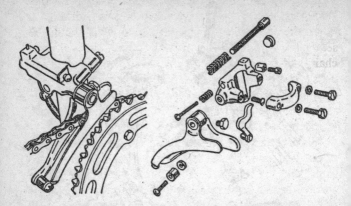

FIGURE 60. Simplex "Prestige" front derailleur mechanism. Parts are shown in approximate position of assembly.

and push both levers up and toward the head tube. This will shorten the cables with little fuss. If only one is short, you will have to go to the far end of the cable—trace it—loosen the locknut, and pull up the slack there.

You may find that your front derailleur control arm doesn't work too well although the stops have been properly set and the arm locates the chain accurately over each of the front chain wheels. If this is so, check the orientation of the front control mechanism. Stand up and look down at it. Notice that the pair of guide arms point to the rear hub. Check to make certain that they point toward its center. If the guide has rotated a bit, you may find that the shift action is faulty or erratic or that the chain runs on the front guide. Correct this by simply loosening the bolt and turning a bit.

The front changer guide may also be too high or too low. Generally all the chain needs is a gentle poke to get it into place. Therefore the guide can be fairly high above the chain wheel. But if front shifting is erratic, try lowering the guide. There is no set position for this guide, and every changer develops its own quirks.

Another adjustment is the rear axle. This should be set square across the frame. If it is not, you will have chain-jumping troubles. If you have the better frame ends, you will have a pair of long set screws which you can adjust so that the axle is held orthogonal to the frame and you need not worry about its slipping. If not, keep checking.

While you are at this end of the cycle, notice whether or not there are any washers between the left side of the frame and the rear hub. It matters little whether there are any or not, so long as the chain and wheel are centered. What matters is that you remember the presence of any. Should you remove the rear wheel, you must return all the washers because they space the wheel properly in the fork. If you have a used cycle and you are having trouble, check this by noting how the chain wheel and rear cogs line up when the axle is square and the tire is centered in the frame. There may be washers missing; add them if necessary to make the parts line up. The chain may stay on with the wheel to one side, but it will add wear and shorten the life of the chain and the gears.

TROUBLES

Taking it for granted that you have read and understood all that has been written so far, here are some of the problems that may beset you in running a derailleur.

No changer action at all. The control cable is broken. The control assembly has slipped so far down the tube that there is no pull left in the cable. Remove slack, replace cable.

Changer action is sluggish. Determine whether it is

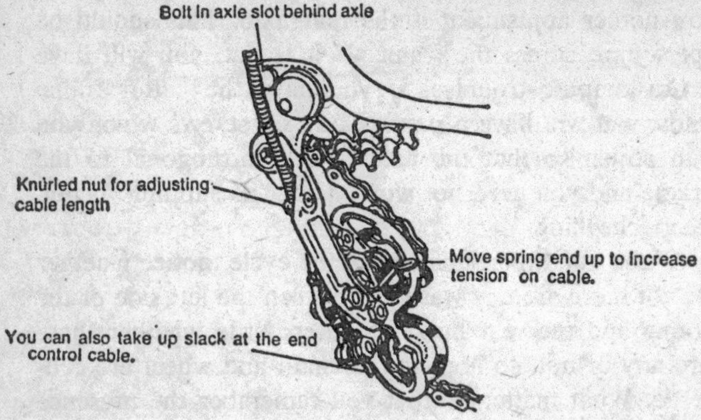

Bolt in axle slot behind axle

Knurled nut for adjusting
cable length

Move spring end up to increase
tension on cable.

You can also take up slack at the end
control cable.

FIGURE 61. Huret "Luxe" rear derailleur mechanism.

the control arm, cable, or changer mechanism that is
sticking. Work control arm rapidly. When you return
arm to upright position, can you see or feel cable slack?
If so, the cable or control is sticking. Loosen the knob
controlling the friction on the control lever. The lever
should be free. If not, disassemble it very carefully,
keeping track of all parts. Wipe clean and wash. Dry
and reassemble. *Do not lubricate.* If rusted, make
smooth with oo emery cloth.

With the tension knob loosened, take hold of the
control lever and the distant end of the cable where it
joins the derailleur mechanism. Tug on the lever and
feel the movement at the cable end. This test will
quickly reveal a cable that is stuck in its housing. If
control lever and cable are free, the trouble is in the
changer mechanism. Try oil on pivot points before
disassembling.

Because of the nature of the pantograph, it is difficult to push or pull on the pantograph to see if it is
sticking. But you can loosen the control lever and pull

on the cable, then hold the arm to one side and see how quickly its spring returns it. You don't have to move the arm its full travel distance, usually, to discover sticky operation.

On some of the derailleur mechanisms it is possible to overtighten a bolt that acts as a pivot and so to lock the mechanism or make it difficult to operate. On all the rear derailleurs lint, threads, and the like are readily caught in the moving wheels and can interfere with the operation of the changer as well as with wheel rotation.

When examining an old derailleur that isn't working properly, look for side play in the pantograph when it is extended. Simply push across the arms lightly to see if there is enough play to permit the arms to catch or stick in operation. When the arms are badly worn, they will not move far enough when the cable is pulled, and so there will be uncertain changes to and from the large rear cog and the outside front chain wheel.

Spring tension should also be checked on an old mechanism. The newer designs have provisions for spring take-up. Look at the end of the spring, and if you have this feature you will see a few indentations. Move the spring end against its natural inclination to another detent notch to increase tensions. If the spring is soft and there is no correction feature, the spring will have to be replaced.

Chain jumps off. Determine first whether the chain jumps from one particular cog or from the high or low end of the gear ratio. If it is one particular cog, that cog may be bent, or it may be loose; though this is unlikely unless its side spaces are filled with soil. If the jumps occur at high speed, with the chain on the smallest rear cog, the jockey is sticking or its tension has been lost or the chain has grown too long. If the jump occurs at very low speed when the chain is on the largest rear and front gear, the chain may not be far enough over to center on these two gears.

If the chain doesn't always climb up on the large front wheel, the chain may be a mite short, there may be too much tension in the jockey, or you may need to set the guide arm a bit past dead center. Sometimes better results are obtained if the chain is directed a mite past the center of the large gear.

Incidentally, the easiest way to lengthen the chain is to permit the rear wheel to come forward a bit. To shorten, move the rear wheel back a fraction.

Should the chain jump off at the same point on the front wheel, the wheel may be bent or a cog on the wheel may be bent. If the chain always jumps off from the front wheel but doesn't appear to leave the wheel at the same point every time, the trouble may be in the chain. There may be a stiff link, or the chain may be badly worn.

If the chain frequently jumps from the rear cogs when you are down-gearing, you may be down-gearing too fast. The chain may be dry and stiff. The jockey wheels may be sticking, so that they cannot swing fast enough to take up the slack. Lubricate.

Noise when pedaling. This can be caused by a dry, worn chain plus kinked-up chain wheels. The chain rattles and bumps as it moves along. Squeaks are generally caused by lack of lube in the idler and guide wheels.

Chain rotates, wheel doesn't. This may be caused by a mirage or in some cases by pawls sticking in an out-of-contact position inside the free-wheel body. The failure of the pawls to engage may be caused by frozen moisture, lack of lubrication, or too much lubrication with grease, which should never be used inside the free wheel.

Try tapping the axle lightly with a hammer. Try waiting for the sun to come out and melt the frost inside the machine, or softening the grease so that the springs can push the pawls into place. In any event, you will need to remove and clean the free wheel sooner or later.

Best do it sooner, before you get stuck permanently out in the woods somewhere.

Worn and bent parts. So far we have assumed that all is fairly shipshape—that you are having trouble with a reasonably new derailleur. More often the troubles will arise from a bent or badly worn derailleur mechanism.

The small idler wheels take a beating. They are small and rotate rapidly, far more rapidly than the wheels. They wear, growing smaller with age, which increases the slack in the chain. When their bearings wear, the jockey wheels may tilt and fail to deliver the chain as directed. This can cause the chain to jump or fail to shift—most often it fails to shift down speed—to a larger gear.

When the joints of the parallelogram or pantograph wear, play develops and the arm will not move as far in response to control-lever movement as before. The arm may wobble and the chain may jump from side to side.

When the parts of the derailleur are bent by one force or another, anything may happen. The first sign is usually noise. You can hear the chain drag. The second sign is malfunction of some kind. Should you suspect a bent mechanism, do not jump right in and straighten it out. The modern derailleur is so kooky that it is difficult to remember what is the correct shape and what is not. Hoist the bike in the air and keep testing and watching until you are certain some part is bent. Then bend it back gently. Should you overbend and have to correct, it may break off.

FREE-WHEEL INSTALLATION AND REMOVAL

A five-speed free wheel consists of six pieces of metal that you can see: the body, inside which are the free-wheel pawls and ratchet and bearings, and the five cogs that go outside.

To install a free-wheel body, start by removing the rear wheel of the cycle. Find the side of the hub with the threads, and grease them lightly to facilitate future free-wheel removal. Then, facing the threaded side of the hub, screw the free-wheel body onto these threads by turning the free-wheel body to the right. Butter the threads on the inside of the gears very lightly with some more grease, then screw the cogs, largest first, onto the free-wheel body. At this point all the parts are screwed finger-tight. You can go ahead and string the chain if you wish. Pedaling acts to tighten all these parts on the hub. To be safe, you can tighten them with a slotted tool for the slotted free-wheel body and the splined tool for the splined body. To make the nubs on the tool fit the slots on the body, finger-tighten an axle nut over the slotted tool and take a wrench to the tool. You can hold the wheel for leverage. The splined tool slips over the axle and into the center of the free wheel. The short splined tools require a wrench; the large ones have a handle. (See Figures 62 and 63.) Incidentally, on some free-wheel designs two or more cogs are screwed onto the body before the body is screwed onto the wheel hub. This will be obvious when you examine it.

We now have the cogs tightly clustered on the body of the free wheel and the free wheel tightly turned up on the hub. The wheel may now be installed. If this is a new installation, the chain will be strung through the derailleur and over the rear cogs. If we have removed a wheel, the chain has not been opened, and we simply slip it over the cogs and center the wheel in the frame before tightening both axle nuts.

To remove the free wheel, we run the chain on the small front and rear gears, push the chain forward and free of the chain wheels, loosen the rear axle nuts, and slip the wheel down and out of the frame. Generally we

Gear cluster

FIGURE 62. The slotted free-wheel removal tool is held in place while used by running the axle nut up on the axle. Hold the wheel and turn the tool to the left to remove the free wheel.

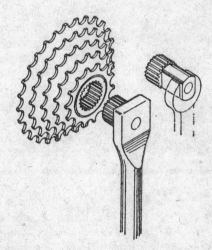

FIGURE 63. Tools for removing free wheels with splined interiors. The small tool needs a wrench.

do not have to touch the derailleur. The same tools mentioned previously—splined tool for splined free wheels and nubbed tools for slotted free wheels—are used. One holds the wheel at the tire and backs the body of the free wheel and the cluster of gears off the hub thread. This is simple enough.

The task of removing the gears from the free-wheel body is not difficult, but it is impossible without the correct tools. You may wish to purchase these tools, but many cyclists find it simpler to let their cycle shop take the free-wheel body apart, clean it, and lubricate it for them. As stated previously, when the outside (small-gear) end of the free wheel is turned up, you can pour some oil into the space and let it seep into the works overnight.

CHAPTER 13

Hub Gears

There are two-, three-, four-, and five-speed hub-gear
systems in use today. The two- and three-speed hub
gears have one control lever which operates a cable that
terminates at a little metal chain, generally at the center
of the right side of the rear hub. Four- and five-speed
hubs generally have a second cable terminating in a second control up front and an angle device, sometimes
called a bell crank, at the center of the left-hand side of
the rear hub.

Some geared hubs provide speed changes only.
Others are combined with coaster brakes. Still other
types have no control cables but are shifted by back-
pedaling.

The speed changes provided vary with manufacturer,
hub design, and to some extent, gear selection. The
manufacturer offers more than one set of gears with a
particular hub.

Hub speed-change controls are similar to derailleur controls in that the cyclist operates a lever up front that moves a cable which effects the gear shift. On the derailleur, the cyclist himself determines how much the lever shall be moved. With a hub gear, the distance the lever is moved is fixed by the lever mechanism. This makes it much simpler for the cyclist, but to some degree more difficult to repair.

The shift lever on the hub-gear set must match the hub gear. One cannot arbitrarily change control mechanisms.

STURMEY ARCHER ADJUSTMENT

If you look at the right-hand end of a Sturmey Archer two- or three-speed hub, you will find a gadget like the one pictured in Figure 64. Before you make any adjustments, make certain the large nut with the hole in its side is on tightly; make certain the little chain is tightly fastened to the rod and that the rod is turned all the way to the right. To turn the rod, pull it out with your fingers and use a pair of pliers on it. Don't apply the pliers to the chain. If you do not have enough rod to grab, remove the nut with the hole. Make the rod snug, but don't overtighten. Put a few drops of oil on the chain. It is steel and will rust.

Check the gear-changer control lever. Put it in its middle position for a three-speed job. Returning to the rear end, loosen the large nut on the end of the control cable. Hold the screw on the cable end with one hand, to loosen the knurled locknut. Look in the little hole. The end of the rod, where it joins the chain, should be in line with the end of the axle as in Figure 64B. If it is not, turn the threaded rod on the end of the control cable to adjust. Then finger-tighten the locknut.

If you wish, you can try another adjustment method.

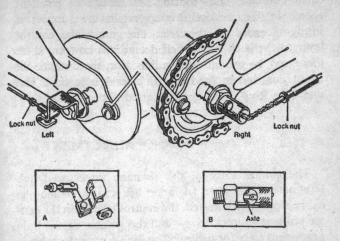

FIGURE 64. Gear adjustments for a five-speed Sturmey Archer hub. These directions hold true for other similar hubs, with the exception of a Shimano. (A) Left control. Place control level in backward position and take up the slack. Tighten the lock nut. (B) Right control. Place control lever in the middle position. Adjust the cable until the end of the rod is flush with the end of the axle. Tighten the lock nut.

Check the nut with the window and the rod on the chain for tightness. Put the speed-control lever in its high position—the position that lets the cable go back the greatest distance. Now check the cable near the knurled locknut. There should be very little tension in the cable, but no slack. To check, loosen the cable at the adjustment until there is some visible slack. Then take it up and tighten the locknut. When the cable is completely released and the inner spring pulls the control rod and its cable inside the hub, the hub is in its highest speed-gear ratio.

On the five-speed Sturmey Archer hub you will find a second control cable on the left side of the hub. This cable terminates in a little angle mounted on a pivot, as shown in Figure 64A. Make certain the support is firmly mounted on the axle. Then push the control lever to the back position, and take up whatever slack there may be present in the cable. If there is any doubt about this, loosen the cable first until it is slack and then take it up, locking the knurled nut afterward.

SHIMANO ADJUSTMENT

The control cable of the Shimano three-speed hub terminates in a little angle or bell crank. When the cable is properly adjusted, the control lever is in the center position—direct drive—and the pointer on the little arm points to N for neutral. The lock nut on the cable is loosened, and the threaded metal arm is turned as required.

TROUBLE-SHOOTING THE HUB CHANGERS

A surprising number of malfunctions can be traced to faulty adjustment. The cable is too tight or too slack. In some instances the control cable can cause speed changes without the control being touched at all. All it takes is some kinks in the cable that act as springs and just enough tension on the cable. The bike frame gives a little, and the cable moves in response to the spring. Should the cable break, most if not all changers will automatically shift into their highest speed.

Generally trouble in the control cable affects the end gear ratios. It is difficult or impossible to get the bike in high or low, but direct drive (center position) works fine. A sticky cable would shift from direct drive to high after a few minutes. A short cable would prevent the mechanism from being changed to low gear.

Some shift failures can be traced to incorrect controls. When this happens, the cyclist is unable to secure the gear changes he wishes even though the lever seems to operate perfectly and the cable is properly adjusted. What is happening is that the lever is not moving the cable the correct amount for that particular hub.

The control levers themselves rarely cause malfunction—unless they have been damaged. When this is the case, it is usually easier in the long run to replace the control. It should be noted that the pressure on the control lever is not the same at all points. More pressure is necessary to pull the cable to the low-gear position. A drop of oil on the control lever once a year or so is all the attention it requires.

Noisy hub operation is usually due to lack of lubrication. Speed-change difficulty that is not traceable to sticky cables or rusted control levers may sometimes be due to overly tight chains and/or bent axles. A tight chain will sometimes make a worn hub very noisy. A loose axle will cause noise and changer malfunction.

Should all of the aforementioned appear to be in good order and the control still fail to deliver the three speeds, (or the two additional speeds on the other side of the hub changer), loosen the control cable until it is completely slack. Then crank the wheel and pull the cable by hand to see if that will give you the gear steps. Put a roll of newspaper against the wheel to provide a drag.

If you can get the three speeds when you operate the cable by hand, but not with the control, you have somehow gotten the wrong control, or its middle position is defective. If you cannot get the changer to go into the speeds it is designed for, something is wrong inside the changer. *This is very rare.* Check to make certain the lock nuts and cones are not coming apart.

Lubricate to make certain it is not merely "stiction" inside the hub. Check to make certain the control rods at the ends of the cable are tight.

The planetary gear system is sturdy and simple. It just about never goes out of whack. Its gear-shift mechanism works on a go-no-go basis. It either delivers the ratio built into it or it doesn't deliver the ratio. Sometimes it shifts back and forth by virtue of changing cable pressure. But the ratio never change. To do so would mean changing the gears inside the hub.

LUBRICATION

The hub gears should be taken apart, cleaned, and greased once a year. This is best done by an experienced bike mechanic. Once a month a little SAE 30 oil is injected into the hub via the oil cup or hole. As previously stated, the quantity is always a compromise. You want enough oil to keep the parts lubricated, but not so much oil that you force or wash the grease out. If you are an occasional rider, one drop or two a month is sufficient. If you ride hundreds of miles a week, better give it a half-teaspoon a month.

If you don't want to go to the trouble and expense of having the bike shop dismantle your hub gears once a year—you may not ride enough to warrant it—there is another alternative. With care you can lubricate the wheel bearings in the rear hub. The other running surfaces can then be lubricated every two or even three years, given their monthly quota of oil.

Remove the rear wheel. Lay it on its side. Using two wrenches, loosen the outer locknut. Back it off an inch or so. Now carefully back the bearing cone out a half-inch or so, keeping the wheel resting on the axle all the time. Put some light grease on your pinkie and force it in and on the ball bearings in the bearing cage. Turn the

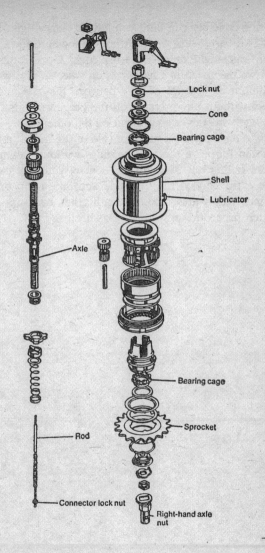

Lock nut

Cone

Bearing cage

Shell

Lubricator

Axle

Bearing cage

Sprocket

Rod

Connector lock nut

Right-hand axle nut

FIGURE 65. Exploded view of a five-speed Sturmey . Archer hub gear.

193

bearing cone back in until you have it finger-tight. Back it off a quarter-turn or so. Bring the locknut down until it is finger-tight on the bearing cone. Go through the drill we discussed in Chapter 8, on wheels. You want a minimum or absence of play between the axle and the wheel without any pressure on the bearings. This done, turn the wheel over and repeat on the other side.

By opening and closing one side of the hub at a time, you can lubricate the axle bearings without risking the works falling out. Actually, of course, you can leave a little extra play in the first side and take it up on the second side—thus fooling with the back-up—and tighten procedure only once per wheel.

CHAPTER 14

Head Sets, Handlebars,
and Seats

Barring spills and other natural disasters, you will probably need to concern yourself with the handlebars and head set no more than once a year when you take the head set apart to clean and grease it, and when you remove old handlebar tape and replace it. Should you fail to clean and regrease the head set at the year's end, fret not. Little harm will be done if you let it go another year, unless you put on thousands of miles each year or race.

HEAD-SET ASSEMBLY

The same basic arrangement of bearings, races, and cones is used in the head set to support the fork as is used in the wheel hubs, pedals, and crank. The top end of the fork—the part that goes into the head tube—is the axle. Its upper end is threaded, and it carries the nut that locks all the parts together. Figure 66 shows the head-set parts without the handlebar stem, which slips inside.

Let us assume you have received a new Cinelli from an unknown admirer (Italian, of course). In addition to the frame and fork, you have on hand a package of all the parts listed at the left of the illustration in Figure 66. These are the assembly steps. Press the upper bearing cone into the top of the head tube. Lay a flat piece of wood across it, and tap it down lightly with a hammer. Now do the same with the lower bearing race, tapping upward this time.

Slip the lower bearing cone over the fork. Spread a layer of grease over the groove in the race. Use a medium-weight grease such as Lubriplate Low Temp or Starfak No. 2. Slip the top of the fork into the head tube, and bring the lower bearing cone close to the race. Press the bearings into the grease in the race. Push the fork all the way up and in. The lower circle of bearings is now in place. Apply grease to the groove in the bearing-race nut. Press the bearings gently into place. Turn the bearing-race nut, bearing side down, and lower it gently over the end of the fork. When you encounter the threads on the form end, turn the nut carefully to the right, making certain you do not cross-thread them. Started correctly, the large nut can be easily tightened with fingers alone. If you cannot turn it with your fingers, back it off and try again. Keep turning the nut all the way to the right until it is finger-tight. Now try turning the fork; it should rotate freely.

Take hold of the fork with one hand and the frame near the head set with the other. Push up on one and down on the other. There should be no play. If there is, try tightening the bearing-race nut with your fingers.

Should you be unable to remove all play with finger tension alone, or should the fork lock in the head tube

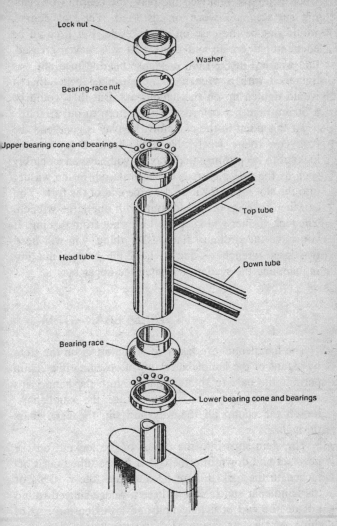

FIGURE 66. Head-set parts and assembly procedure.

when you have removed the play, the bearings or bearing surfaces are worn or distorted. This, of course, would not be the case on a new cycle. But it could be encountered on an old cycle that was never greased, that was left in the rain, or whose bearing-race nut was tightened with a wrench in the mistaken belief that it would tighten up on the handlebars. But that would be a bike of another color, so let us return to our Cinelli.

At this point in the assembly, all play is gone and the fork can rotate freely. Now we have to lay on the locknut to keep things that way. If you have an assembly such as the one pictured, fit the little nib in the washer into the slot made for it on the pipe end of the fork. You can then take up on the locknut with one large wrench. The lock washer will keep the lower nut from turning. If you have the ordinary flat washer thing, you will need two large wrenches—one to hold the bottom nut immobile, and the second to tighten the upper nut.

HANDLEBAR STEM

The handlebars are fastened to the offset on the stem by means of the handlebar clamp. Loosening this clamp permits the bars to rotate; you can turn the hand grips up or down. If you wish to change the handlebars, loosen the clamp all the way and slip the handlebars through.

The stem slips into the center of the locknut on the head set and down into the center of the tube that is attached to the fork. Figure 67 illustrates the working of the handlebar stem. You will see a wedge-shaped round nut on the end of a long bolt and an extension sort of thing which engages a slot in the stem. When the wedge-shaped nut, called the expander nut, is all the way down, you can easily slip the stem into the top of the head set. With the stem in the position you

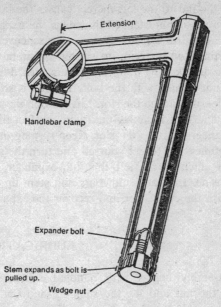

FIGURE 67. Handlebar stem with expander nut. Tightening the bolt pulls the expander nut upward and locks the stem to the fork tube.

wish—handlebars straight across and at your desired height—the nut at the top of the stem is tightened to the right. The expander bolt is pulled up and wedges the stem inside the fork's upper tube. The handlebars are now tight. Incidentally, don't make the expander bolt so tight the stem is permanently deformed or so tight it is impossible for the handlebars to turn out of position at all. You want a little give here should you take a spill and land on the end of your handlebars. Make them tight, but not locked forever.

Let us consider the misfortunes that befall expanders and their bolts. Sometimes, when you are attempting to loosen a handlebar from its fork, you will find that turning the nut to the left merely causes the bolt to rise from the top of the stem. This means the expander nut is stuck. Tap it down lightly with a hammer.

Sometimes when trying to tighten the stem you turn and turn and nothing happens. This is caused by the expander nut turning with the bolt. The nut is so low that its nib doesn't engage the slot. Lift the bolt up with your fingers, and turn it slowly until you can feel the nib on the expander slip into the slot. Keep turning until tight.

Sometimes you forget yourself and turn the stem-bolt head so much to the left that the expander nut falls down inside. Lift the handlebars and stem up and out. Then turn the cycle over and recover the expander nut.

LUBRICATION

Disassembly begins with handle-bar-stem removal. Loosen the nut and lift the stem up and out. Loosen and remove the head-set locknut. Loosen the bearing-race nut just a little. The next steps may be easier if you remove the front wheel and lay the cycle on its side, because unless your bearings are caged, they are going to tumble out when you lower the fork out of the head tube. As with the hubs and cranks, you have got to be alert and catch all the bearings. They are cleaned, along with cages, if any, and the rest of the bearing surfaces including the parts that are pressed into the head tube—the upper bearing cone and the lower bearing race. If you cannot pull them out with your fingers, insert a sawn-off broomstick handle into the head tube and use the square end to gently pry the parts out. Don't try to do it all at once; tap each side of the circular part lightly.

After washing the running parts in kerosine or

gasoline, regrease and reassemble. Again, be careful not to over-tighten the bearing cones.

HANDLEBARS

If you use grips on your handlebars, you need not concern yourself with the end of the handlebar tube. The ends are safely covered. If you don't use grips, you should insert handlebar end plugs whether you use tape or not.

Tape provides a firm, dry, warm gripping surface. The taped handlebar is more comfortable on a long ride because you have so much more choice of hand position than merely the grips. And the bare metal is slippery and very cold in the winter.

Tape is applied by starting with several turns at a spot near the center of the bars. This locks the tape in place. Then one progresses at an angle until the end of the bar is reached, going around the hand-brake bracket. At the end of the bar, the end of the tape is stuffed into the inside of the tube, and a plug is driven into the tube atop the tape to hold it fast.

There are several kinds of tape on the market, some with adhesive backing and some without. I prefer the no-stickum cotton tape. It is more difficult to wrap but absorbs moisture and provides a better grip than either rubber or plastic stickum tapes.

SEATS

Seats may be raised or lowered a number of inches by loosening the bolt on the seat-tube portion of the frame. Since seat posts are available in lengths to fifteen inches and perhaps longer, it is possible to vary seat height by thirteen inches on a standard bike frame, as differentiated from a folding bike frame. Thirteen inches is given as the limiting increase in height because you should have two inches of seat post within the seat tube at a minimum, and preferably a bit more.

All seats can be moved forward and backward to some degree. If you have a common, everyday seat post shaped like a "7," you can move the seat the length of the horizontal section of the "7," bearing in mind that the full width of the clamp must remain on the post. If you have a racing post, which may simply be a single straight tube of metal, you can slide the seat forward and backward as far as the wire frame section of the seat permits, and no more. Should you have a Campagnolo or similar seat post, you will have a clamp atop the post which clamps to the wire frame of the seat, but you will still be limited to the horizontal section of the wire frame.

The third adjustment common to all seats—or saddles, as they are called most often by cyclists—is tilt. Seats can be tilted up or down to some degree. The degree of possible tilt varies with post design, clamp design, seat design, and their combination. The old-design, low-priced seats could only be tilted by sliding the seat forward or backward all the way until the curved portion of the wire frame was in the clamp. The clamp was fixed in the matter of tilt. With such seats a downward tilt means the seat is moved back a bit. An upward tilt of the nose of the saddle requires that the seat be moved all the way forward in the clamp.

None of these adjustments pose any problem to the cyclist armed with wrenches of the proper size. The problems you may run into are these. You cannot tighten the seat post. It keeps slipping down. Lose weight, or replace the seat post. Do not give the binder bolt on the frame your all. You may strip it and then it will need to be hacksawed off. Instead look at the rear

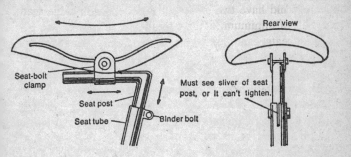

Seat-bolt
clamp

Seat post

Seat tube

Binder bolt

Rear view

Must see sliver of seat
post, or it can't tighten.

FIGURE 68. Seat adjustment. Loosening the binder bolt permits vertical seat-post adjustment. Loosening the seat-bolt clamp permits tilt adjustment as well as forward and backward adjustment when the post is shaped like a "7."

of the seat tube, where the binder bolt lies. See if there is a sliver of bright seat-post metal showing, as illustrated in Figure 68. Its presence indicates you have a seat post of the correct diameter or thickness. If there is no visible space between the edges of the slot in the seat tube, the slot is completely closed; the seat post is too thin for that seat tube. Someone goofed. Get the next thicker seat post. You want the one that just makes it when the binder nut is loose. Go to a bike shop where you can actually try several posts.

If the seat tube is not completely closed and the seat still slides down, chances are that someone oiled the seat post. Loosen the binder bolt; remove and wipe the post dry. Run a rag down the inside of the seat tube to clean that. Then wrap some sandpaper around the bottom of the seat post, and holding the sandpaper firm in one hand, revolve the post. This will produce a fine cross line on the post. Wipe clean and try again.

CHAPTER 15

Frames

As long as the bike's frame is not kicked, stepped on, or bashed into, it will last indefinitely. The frame doesn't wear. When it does suffer contusions, it can be straightened when the damage is not too severe. When any tube is deformed to the point where it has closed, the tube is gone. With an expensive frame you can have your favorite little silversmith unsolder the joints and insert a new section of tubing. If the frame is not joined by lugs, there is nothing to be done except make an unsightly patch by brazing a curved fish plate to either side of the damaged area.

CORRECTING DENTED TUBES

When the dent in the tubing is very shallow, you can ignore it; it will not rob the frame of much strength. If the frame member is bent in a curve, do not put your knee to it. Instead lay the part down on a flat board and gently press the metal flat. Then lay two strips of wood a distance to either side of the bend and press again. If pressing won't do it, lay a heavy timber—two by six, or similar thickness of wood—at least a foot long over the dented portion of the tube and bang on that. A small sledge will help. You want slow, heavy blows. Don't rap the pipe directly with a hammer; you will mash it.

Never put a torch to a badly bent section to straighten it out. This can be done, but you will remove the metal's temper and change it from steel to very weak strap iron.

REPAINTING

The auto-parts supply houses carry dozens of touch-up paints in small bottles fitted with paint brushes. The chance that any of the complex modern auto colors will match the color of your cycle is slim. However, even a daub of mis-matched color is better than a rust spot. The rust itself does little harm, but it is unsightly.

Whether you plan eventually to repaint your entire cycle or not, you must make certain there is no wax or grease—as from frequent hand contact—on a spot to be touched up; also see that there is no rust. If you are planning to repaint, rub the spot bright and smooth with oooo sandpaper. If you are just going to touch up, any fine sandpaper will do. Apply the paint with the metal at 70° F. or warmer, let it dry, and it's done.

Repainting the entire frame is not difficult, but it does take time and care. With sufficient care, you can duplicate the original factory paint job. The cost of the materials necessary for repainting is less than five dollars.

Disassemble the cycle. Remove all parts until you have the frame free. Take a rag and remove all the grease and oil that may have collected on the ends of the frame; the fork tips, top and bottom of the head tube, fork crown, and bottom bracket. Devise a gadget to hold the front fork in an upright position. You might cut a hole in an old bench and insert the fork into the hole. You might assemble some clean bricks to hold the fork upright and immobile. Devise another gadget, such

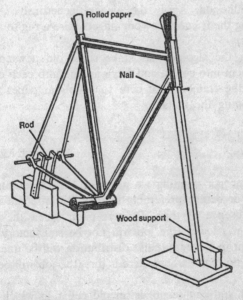

FIGURE 69. Repainting the frame. Pieces of scrap lumber will hold the frame upright; rolled papers will seal the frame apertures.

as the one pictured in Figure 69, to hold the frame upright and clear of the ground.

To strip the old paint you will need about a pint of Red Devil or similar paint remover. Apply it with an old, clean brush, or a cheap new brush, let stand, and wipe clean with a rag. Use a piece of wood to scrape off the old paint if necessary, but don't use a metal tool because it will scratch the metal. Repeat the remover application and wipe off until metal is completely free of paint. Then wash the frame and fork in alcohol. Do not use rubbing alcohol, because it contains too much water and bay rum. Antifreeze alcohol is no good either; it may contain gylcerin, which will interfere with paint adhesion. Apply the alcohol generously. Avoid touching the frame with your fingers. Use a rag to make contact.

After the alcohol bath, take some old newspapers, twist them into cones, and force a cone into each opening in the frame. Take care to keep the paper from overlapping the metal.

SPRAYING

For proper painting we need an air temperature at 70° F. or better (preferably better), still air, and complete absence of dust. Do not paint when the temperature is lower (the job will not be satisfactory), do not paint in a breeze (paint distribution will be uneven), and do not paint where there is dirt (the job will be terrible).

If all you can secure is an old cellar in which coal was once used for fuel—don't paint. It will be horrible. If you have a reasonably clean basement or garage, hose the floor and walls down and paint soon after. You should do the same if you are painting outdoors on a driveway.

The first coat of paint should be a primer. Use the same primer that is used for auto-body work. You can purchase it in a small pressure can in an auto-parts store. Make certain you have shaken it until you are a bit dizzy. Make certain the can is not cool to the touch. in which case the paint temperature may be low. Leave it in a warm spot overnight, or place it in a saucepan of warm water for an hour or so. Shake it crazy again. Apply the primer carefully, using the following technique.

Point the can away from the target. Bring the can about eight to ten inches from the metal. Press the button. The initial spray will not hit the metal. Now, with the spray going, swing your arm past the work. Keep the button down until the spray is to one side of the metal. Remove your finger and repeat. To do a good job the can must be moving all the time paint is emerging. Take care to see that your finger does not overlap the button. If it does, you may get drops forming on the work.

Hold the can close enough to the work to produce a wet painted surface. But not so close you get drips. If you see a drip, forget it. Unless the concentration of paint is very heavy, it will smooth itself.

Continue applying primer until all the metal is covered. Now clear the nozzle by turning the can upside down, pressing the button up until the spray is all air. If you do not do this, the paint will seal the orifice, and you can throw the balance of the paint away.

Wait several hours. Give the primer plenty of time to harden. Now rub it down with automotive type-400 sandpaper. Start with dry paper, which cuts better. Then wet the paper down. Use a dish of water, and dip the paper as you work. This produces the smoothest possible surface with the paper. If the primer surface is rough, start with coarse paper, say 100, and then wipe dry with alcohol and spray it again. Repeat with finer paper and then the wet paper until you have a perfectly smooth surface which is almost but not quite shiny. The paint will make it shine.

Now apply the paint. Follow the same technique. Watch the overspray. Take care that paint that misses the front of the cycle doesn't strike the rear parts. The droplets will be dry and form a rough, granular surface. Give the cycle three or four coats at a minimum, with plenty of drying time in between. Wait at least a week before applying protective wax.

FILLING DENTS

Shallow dents and gouges can be hidden from sight with auto putty. Clean and prime the area as directed. Next, apply thin coatings of putty to the dented area with a squeegee, or a soft piece of wood. The thinner the coating, the more quickly it will harden. When the depression is filled and the putty has thoroughly dried, use a file or coarse sandpaper on a block of wood to bring the putty level with the adjacent metal surface. Wipe free of putty dust, and apply a very thin layer of putty to fill the file and/or sandpaper marks. Dry and sand with increasingly finer paper until you are working with 400 paper. Clean, prime, and paint.

Cycle supply houses

Ron Kitching
Hookstone Park
Harrogate, England
Catalogue, interesting and informative, $3.

WheelGoods Corporation
2737 Hennepin Avenue
Minneapolis, Minnesota 55408
Catalogue, interesting and informative, $2.

Big Wheel, Ltd.
340 Holly Street
Denver, Colorado 80220
Catalogue, interesting, informative, somewhat similar to
   WheelGoods' publication, $2.

Cyclo-Pedia
311 North Mitchell Avenue
Cadillac, Michigan 49601
Catalogue, interesting and informative, $1.

(Some carry cycles and parts.)
L. L. Bean, Inc.
Freeport, Maine 04032
Top-flight equipment, similar prices.
Catalogue is free for asking.

I. Goldberg and Sons
429 Market Street
Philadelphia, Pennsylvania 19106
Good equipment, competitive prices.
Free 150-page camping catalogue.

Colorado Outdoor Sports Corporation
P.O. Box 5544
Denver, Colorado 80217
Some unusual items for camping.
Excellent, free catalogue.

Bike Riders Aids
Holdsworthy Company, Ltd.
London, S.E. 20, England
Considerable savings if purchased there.
At last query, catalogue is still free.

Cycling organizations

Amateur Bicycle League of America
4233 205th Street
Bayside, Long Island, New York
This is the governing body of American cycling; a member of the U.S. Olympic Committee.

Bicycle Institute of America
122 E. 42nd Street
New York, New York 10011
Bike manufacturers', distributors', etc., association. Excellent source of general cycling information.

League of American Wheelmen, Inc.
5118 Foster Avenue
Chicago, Illinois 60630

Probably the most active cycle club in this country. Has members in forty-five states. Membership is a must for anyone truly interested in the sport.

International Bicycle Touring Society
846 Prospect Street
LaJolla, California 92037
Conducts worldwide bycle tours.

Cycling periodicals

Bicycling
234 Montgomery Street
San Francisco, California 94104
America's only nondealer-oriented cycle magazine.
Subscription, $6 a year.

Cycle Touring
69 Meadrow, Godalming
Surrey, England
Good overseas cycling information, though written for English cyclists.
Write for present subscription rate.

Cycling and Sporting Cyclists
161-166 Fleet Street
London, E.C. 4, England
For the racing enthusiast; a weekly.
Subscription $16.50 a year.

Local AYH offices

Arizona
   Arizona State Council
   4634 E. Lewis Avenue
   Phoenix 85008

California
   Golden Gate Council
   625 Polk Street
   San Francisco 94102

Los Angeles Council
318 N. La Brea Avenue
Los Angeles 90036

Northern California Council
P.O. Box 15649
Sacramento 95813

San Diego Council
7850 Eads Avenue
LaJolla 92037

San Gabriel Valley Council
215 West 1st Street
Claremont 91711

Connecticut
Fairfield County Council
P.O. Box 173, Southport 06490

Hartford Area Council
YMCA, 315 Pearl Street
Hartford 06103

New Haven Council
48 Howe Street
New Haven 06511

District of Columbia
Potomac Area Council
1501 16th Street, N.W.
Washington D.C. 20036

Illinois
Metropolitan Chicago Council
2210 N. Clark Street
Chicago 60614

Massachusetts
Greater Boston Council
251 Harvard Street
Brookline 02146

Michigan
 Metropolitan Detroit Council
 14335 West McNichols Road
 Detroit 48235

Minnesota
 Minnesota Council
 P.O. Box 9511
 Minneapolis 55440

Missouri
 Lewis & Clark Council
 12201 Blue River Road
 Kansas City 64146

 Ozark Area Council AYH
 P.O. Box 13099
 St. Louis 63119

Nebraska
 Nebraskaland Council
 2740 A Street
 Lincoln 65802

New York
 Metropolitan New York Council
 535 West End Avenue
 New York, N. Y. 10024

 Syracuse Council
 735 S. Beech Street
 Syracuse 13210

Ohio
 Columbus Council
 P.O. Box 3165
 Columbus 43210

 Lake Erie Council
 2000 Terminal Tower
 Cleveland 44113

Lima Council
Box 173
Lima 45802

Toledo Area Council
5320 Fern Drive
Toledo 43613

Pennsylvania
Delaware Valley Council, AYH Inc.
4714 Old York Road
Philadelphia 19141

Pittsburgh Council
6300 Fifth Avenue
Pittsburgh 15232

Wisconsin
Wisconsin Council
P.O. Box 233
Hales Corners 53130

INDEX

Air pumps, hand-operated, 86
Airing tires, 113-115
Alcohol, antifreeze, 208
Alignment, frame, 46
All-metal pedals, 62, 63
Amateur Bicycle League of America, 212
American-style pedals, 154-155
American Youth Hostel, 33-34
local offices (by state), 213-216
Antitheft suggestions, 81-82
Auto-type tube patches, 101

Backpacks, 32

Bad weather, avoiding cycling in, 23
Ball bearings
basic arrangement, 78
care of, 76-78
lubrication, 71-72
Balloon tires, 38, 47-48, 96-104
basic principle of, 97
construction of, 97
finding location of leak, 97-99
mounting, 107
removing from rim, 100
repairing, 98-104
wear, 97
Battery lights, 63-64
Bean, L. L., Inc., 212

Beginners, *see* Learning to ride
Bendix coaster brakes, 144, 145, 146
Bicycle Institute of America, 212
Bicycling (periodical), 213
Big Wheel, Ltd., 211
Bike Riders Aids (supply house), 212
Bike size
  frame and, 40-42
  learning to ride, 8-10
  reach distance, 42
  selecting, 37-44
Bottom bracket bearing wrench, 87
Brakes, 13, 133-149
  adjusting shoe height, 136, 137
  adjusting shoe-to-rim clearance, 135, 136-8
  cable replacement, 139-140
  cable-tube replacement 140-141
  caliper arms (opening or closing), 137
  care of, 81
  center-pull caliper, 61
  inspection, 134-136
  lubrication, 148-149
  normal wear of, 136
  off-center, 144
  oiling, 81
  removing wheel and, 122-123
  selecting, 60-61
  shoes
    height adjustment, 136
  inspection, 134-135
    replacing, 138-139
    -to-rim clearance, 135, 136-138
    uneven wear, 144

  sticky, how to cure, 141-144
  See also Hand brakes; Pedal brakes

C spanner, 87
Cable replacement, 139-140
Cable-tube replacement, 140-141
Cadmium cells, 64
Caliper arms, opening or closing, 137
Caliper brakes
  center-pull, 60, 61
  control of, 60
  front, 122-123
Camping, 29-35
  age group and, 30
  compared to touring, 31-32
  gear, 32
  maximum load per cycle, 32
  meaning of, 31
  objective, 30
  points to consider, 29-31
  quitting time, 31
  supply houses, 212
Capo Berta (handlebar design), 57
Care, 65-83
  antitheft suggestions, 81-82
  bearing mechanisms, 76-78
  chains, 79
  derailleurs, 79-80
  external, 66-67
  inspection, 68-70
  lubricants and lubrication, 71-76
  pedals, 80
  storage, 82-83
  tires, 110-113
  See also Repairs

217

Center-pull caliper brakes, 60, 61
Chains, 161-169
    antitheft suggestions, 80-81
    care, 79
    and chain wheels, 161-169
    cleaning and lubrication, 75
    coaster-brake, 161
    crank troubles, 170
    derailleur, 161, 164-169
    inspection, 69, 70
    length of, 161, 165-169
    meaning of, 161
    nonderailleur, 163-164
    offset and force-fit rivet connectors, 163-164
    pitch, width, and length, 161-162
    rivet extractor, 89, 163
    removal, 162-164
    slack test, 70
    spring-connecting arrangement, 162-163
    wear, 165
    wheels, 169
Cleats, shot, 62-63
Clincher tires, 47, 48-49, 104, 105, 107
    basic principle of, 97
    cost of, 49
    mounting, 105, 107
    punctures in, 105
    removing from rim, 100
    repair and care, 50
    replacing, 105
    rim cross sections, 49
Clothing
    for learning to ride, 10
    safety, 26-27
    what to avoid, 27
Coaster brakes, see Pedal brakes
Colorado Outdoor Sports

Corporation, 212
Cranks, 155-160
    assembly, 159-160
    basic configurations, 155
    chain troubles, 170
    cottered and cotterless, 155-160
    hangers, cleaning and lubricating, 75
Curbstone, driving over, 24
Cycle Touring (periodical), 213
Cycles
    brakes, 133-149
    care, 65-83
    chains and chain wheels, 161-169
    cost of, 37
    derailleurs, 171-186
    frames, 205-210
    handlebars, 198-201
        stems, 198-200, 201
    head-set assembly, 195-198
    hub gears, 187-194
    learning to ride, 7-17
    organizations, 212-213
    pedals, and cranks, 151-160
    periodicals, 213
    repairs, 85-92
    safety, 19-28
    seats, 201-203
    selecting, 37-64
    supply houses, 211-212
    tires, 93-116
    touring and camping, 29-36
    types of, 37-40
    wheels, 117-132
Cycling and Sporting Cyclists (periodical), 213
Cyclo-Pedia (supply house), 211

Delivery cycles, 37
Derailleurs, 50, 51, 171-186
    adjustments, 176-179
    care, 79-80
    chain, 161, 164-169
        jumps off, 181
        rotates, wheel doesn't,
            182
    changer action sluggish,
        179-180
    changing the chain, 175-
        176
    cleaning and lubrication,
        75, 79-80
    control cable, 174-175
    free wheel
        installation and
            removals, 183-186
        parts, 172
    front and rear mechanism,
        172-176
    front control arm, 178-179
    inspection, 69
    jockey wheels, 175
    meaning of, 173
    no changer action, 179
    noise when pedaling, 182
    and overtightening bolts,
        181
    rear-axle adjustment, 179
    rear mechanism, 172-173
    shifting, 16-17
    spring take-up, 181
    taking up slack in, 177-
        178
    worn and bent parts, 183
Dished wheels, treating, 130-
    131
Dismounting, 14
Double-butted frames, 45-46
Drive chains, connecting
    ends of, 162

European-style pedals, 152-
    153

Extensions, handlebar, 58-59
External care, 66-67

Folding cycles, 37
Food, before cycling, 25
Frames, 205-210
    alignment, 46
    bike size and, 40-41
    centering wheel in, 124
    computing size of, 43
    correcting dented tubes,
        205-206
    double butting process, 46
    filling dents, 209-210
    joined by lugs, 45-46
    judging type of, 44-45
    major dimensions, 41
    repainting, 206-207
    selecting, 44-45
    spraying, 208-209
    stripping old paint, 207-
        208
    types of, 45-46
    washing down, 67
Free wheels
    cleaning and lubrication,
        75
    soaking in kerosine, 80
    tools for removing, 185
Front hubs, cleaning and
    lubrication, 75
Front wheels, removing, 122-
    123

Gear changers, types of, 16-
    17
Gear-in-hub speed changer,
    50-51
Gear ratios, 51-56, 57
    choosing, 54-56
    finding, 53-54
    selecting, 51-53
    suggested tables, 55, 57
    for 26- and 27-inch
        wheels, 54

Generator lights, 23
Gold Seal (grease,) 73, 155
Goldberg and Sons, I., 212
GI (government-issued) OG-OO (grease), 73
Green Turtle (cleaning mixture), 67
Group riding, single file, 21

Hacking cycles, 38
Hand brakes, 133-134
  care, 69
  cleaning and lubrication, 75
  control of, 60
  effectiveness of, 133
  inspection, 134-135
  positioning on racing cycle, 134
  testing hand-lever, 134-135
  types of, 61
Handlebars, 198-201
  carrying someone on, 25
  designs, 58
  extensions, 58-59
  inspection, 70
  mounted hand brakes, 133
  rubber grips, 58
  selecting, 57-58
  stems, 198-200, 201
    disassembly, 200-201
    examples of, 59
    with expander nut, 199
    lubrication, 200-201
  tape for, 201
Head-set assembly, 195-198
  cleaning and lubrication, 75
Health precautions, 25
Hitching ride behind truck, 24
Hosteler, The (publication), 34
Hosteling, 33-34

sleeping accommodations, 33
Hub changers
  advantages of, 50-51
  models, 50
  shifting, 16-17
  trouble-shooting, 190-192
Hub gears, 187-194
  cleaning and lubrication, 75, 191, 192
  control levers, 190-191,
  disassembly, 124-125
  end gear ratios, 190
  inspection, 68
  reassembly, 125-126
  removing, 192
  shift failures, 190-191
  shift lever on, 188
  Shimano adjustment, 190
  speed-change controls, 188
  speed-change difficulty, 191
  Sturmey Archer adjustment, 188-190
  systems in use, 187
Huret derailleurs, 174
Huret dual-control levers, 177
Huret "Luxe" rear derailleur mechanisms, 180

Inspection care, 68-70
International Bicycle Touring Society, 213

Jogging, 8

Kerosine, 76
Kitching, Ron (supply house), 211

League of American Wheelmen, Inc., 212
Learning to ride, 7-17
220

balance exercise, 10-11
bike size and, 8-9
braking, 13
clothes to wear, 10
correct positions, 14-15
dismounting, 14
pedaling, 11, 12, 15, 16, 17,
shifting, 16-17
shoe clips and straps, 16
taking off, 10-16
training wheels, 9-10
turning the wheel, 11-12
without fear, 9
Left-hand threads, 89-90
Left-hand turns, 20-21
Lights, 23, 63-64
at night, 23
state-law requirements, 20
Lubrication, 71-73
ball-bearing assemblies, 71
brakes, 148-149
chains, 75
derailleurs, 75
equipment, 73-74
hand brakes, 75
handlebar stems, 201
head sets, 75
hub gear, 75, 190-191, 192, 193
oil holes and covers, 72
pedals brakes, 75
procedure, 76
schedule, 74-76
types of, 73-74
Lubriplate (grease), 155
Low Temp, 74, 196
Type A, 73
Lugs, frames joined by, 45-46

Maes (handlebar design), 57-58
Molykote G (grease), 73
Mud adhesion, reducing, 66

Night riding, safety, 23
Nonderailleur chains, 163
Non-double-butted frames, 46

Off-center brakes, 144
Open-end wrenches, 86
Ovality, curing, 127-131
Overexertion, 25

Panniers, 32
Partially double-butted frames, 46
Pedal brakes (coaster brakes), 144-148
chains, 161-162
cleaning and lubrication, 75
control of, 60
cracking and grinding noises, 148
how they work, 145
inspection, 69
oiling, 81
wear characteristics, 147-148
wheel wobble, 148
Pedal cranks, inspection care, 69
Pedal spanners, 87
Pedaling
learning how, 11-12, 16
trousers for, 26-27
Pedals, 151-155
all-metal, 62-63
American-style (disassembly), 154-155
care, 80
cleaning and lubrication, 75, 80
construction, 151
European-style (disassembly), 152-154
frame size and, 41
inspection, 69

221

and learning to ride, 11, 15, 16, 17
replacing, 152
selecting, 62-63
and shifting, 17
taping blocks of wood to, 42
Pista (handlebar design), 58
Pneumatic tires, 47, 93-96
removing from rim, 96
repairing, 93-96
Pressure, air, 113-115
tire size and, 114
Pressure oil cans, 86
Pressure oilers, use of, 74
Presta (European) tire valves, 97
Puddles, avoiding, 20

Quick-release skewer (lever) mechanism, 118, 119

Racing cycles, 39-40
cost of, 39
Racing shoes with cleats, 63
Raleigh cycles, 139
Randonneur (handlebar design), 58
Rat-trap pedals, 62, 63
Reach, the, 41
computing, 43, 44
distance (front of seat to handlebars), 42-43
handlebar setting to, 59
Rear-axle adjustment, 179
Rear hubs, cleaning and lubrication, 75
Rear wheels
inspection, 69
removing, 122-123
Red Devil (paint remover), 208
Reflectors, 23, 64
state-law requirements, 20
Repairs, 85-92

frozen parts, **91**
guiding principle for, 92
overtightening and, 91
tips on turning boots, 89-90
tools, 86-89
using wrong tool, 91
Reynolds 531 (frame), 46
Right-hand threads, 89-90
Right-hand turns, 20
Rims
curing wobble and ovality, 127-131
positioned by spoke adjustment over hubs, 128
Rubber cement, 109
Rubber grips, handlebar, 58

Saddle height, computing, 43-44
SAE 5 oil, 80
SAE 30 oil, 73, 80, 149, 192
SAE 90 oil, 79
Safety, 19-28
avoiding bad weather, 23-24
clothing, 26
health precautions, 25
at night, 23
obeying the law, 20-21
signal turns, 20, 21
and stupidity, 24-25
traffic, 21-22
watching the road, 20
Schrader (American) tire valves, 95
Schrader valve stems, 94, 95
Seats, 201-203
adjustments, 202-203
moving forward and backward, 202
raising or lowering, 202
seltcting, 61
tightening post, 202-203

tilt, 202-203
Selecting cycle, 37-64
  brakes, 60-61
  frames, 44-45
  gear ratio, 51-52
  handlebars, 57-58
    extensions, 58-59
  lights, 63, 64
  pedals, 62, 63
  and ratio, finding, 53-54
  seats, 61
  size, 40-44
  speed changers, 50-52
  tires, 47-50
  type of, 37-40
  wheels, 46-47
Serial numbers, 82
Sewer covers, avoiding, 20
Shifting, 16-17
Shimano adjustment, 190
Shoe clips and straps, 16
Signal turns, 20
Simonize (cleaning mixture), 67
Simplex "Prestige" front derailleur mechanism, 178
Slotted free-wheel removal tool, 185
Speed changers
  how gearing works, 52
  kinds of, 50
  purpose of, 50
  selecting, 50-51
Spokes
  nipples keys, 87
  stainless-steel, 47
  wheel wobble and, 127-131
  wrenches, 86
  See also Wheels
Standard Milremo rat-trap pedals, 62
Starfak No. 2 (grease), 74, 196

Steering head pliers, 87
Sticky brakes, 141-144
Stillson wrench, use of, 86
Stop signals, hand, 21
Storage space, 82-83
Stunt riding, 24
Sturmey Archer hubs, 188-189, 192
Supply houses, list of, 211-212

Tailgating cars, 21
Taking off, 10-16
  for beginners, 12
  correct and incorrect positions, 15
Tape, handlebar, 201
Taylor, Major, 58-59
Thorn catchers, 112
Tires, 93-116
  airing, 113-115
  balloon, 38, 47, 96-104, 105, 107
  care, 110-113
  centering, 102
  clinchers, 47, 48, 49, 50, 97, 100, 104-105, 107
  inspection, 68
  irons, 86
  kinds of, 47-48
  pneumatic, 47, 93-96
  pressure gauge, 86
  punctures, 47
  for racing cycles, 39
  selecting, 47-50
  size and air pressure, 114
  tubular, 47-50, 107-110, 111
Toe clips and straps, 62
Tools, 86-89
Touring, 29-35
  age group and, 29-30
  bikes, 38-39
    cost of, 39
    major parts of, 39

weight of, 38-39
for city dwellers, 34-35
compared to camping, 31-32
decision for, 31-34
meaning of, 31
objective, 30-31
and overreaching, 31
quitting time, 31
reservations, 32
Traffic safety, 21-22
Training wheels, 9-10
Tricycles, 37
Tube patches, auto-type, 101
Tubular tires, 47-50, 107-111
  adapters, 49-50
  cost of, 49
  fitting to a wheel, 111
  maximum clincher pressure, 48
  mounting, 109-110
  pounds per square inch, 48
  pressure specifics, 114
  repair and care, 50, 107-112
  rim cross sections, 48
Turns, on narrow roads, 21-22

Underclothing, 26-27

Velox compound, 99
Vidration and shakes (wheel), 119-121

Wax, use of, 66-67
Weinmann "Vainqueur 999" center-pull rear brake, 142

WheelGoods Corporation, 211
Wheels, 117-132
  basic bearing system, 117-119
  best position for, 121
  centering in the frame, 123
  checking side play, 122
  coaster brake drag, 60
  construction, 47
  cross-sectional view of hub, 118
  curing wobble and ovality, 127-131
  external care, 66-67
  fitting tubular tire to, 111
  hub disassembly, 124-125
  hub reassembly, 125-126
  inspection, 68
  lifting, and jumping curb, 24
  removal, 122-124
  rotational freedom, 122
  selecting, 46-47
  squeaks, 119
  thorn catchers, 112
  troubles, 119-122
  wobble, 120, 121, 122, 127-31, 147

Youth Hostels, 33-34
  local offices (by state) 213-216
  membership card, 34

Zeus "Gran Sport" precision-machined hub front, 118